Life *in the* Press
Reflections on Family...

by **Rifka Rosenwein**

with a **foreword** *by* **Tova Mirvis**
and an **introduction** *by* **Robert Goldblum**

Ben Yehuda Press
Teaneck, New Jersey

LIFE IN THE PRESENT TENSE ©2007 Rifka Rosenwein. All rights reserved. No part of this book may be used or reproduced in any manner whatsoever without written permission except in the case of brief quotations embodied in critical articles and reviews.

Published by Ben Yehuda Press
430 Kensington Road
Teaneck, NJ 07666

http://www.BenYehudaPress.com

For permission to reprint, including distribution of the material in this book as part of a synagogue or school newsletter, please contact:
Permissions, Ben Yehuda Press,
430 Kensington Road, Teaneck, NJ 07666.
permissions@BenYehudaPress.com.

Ben Yehuda Press books may be purchased for educational, business, or sales promotional use. For information, please contact:
Special Markets, Ben Yehuda Press,
430 Kensington Road, Teaneck, NJ 07666.
markets@BenYehudaPress.com.

ISBN 0-9789980-4-9
ISBN13 978-0-9789980-4-2
CIP pending

preview edition
07 08 09   / 10 9 8 7 6 5 4 3 2 1

For Akiva
　Meir
　Miriam

With Love

Contents

Foreword by Tova Mirvis	v
Introduction by Robert Goldblum	viii
Acknowledgements	xix

The Home Front

On Marrying Jessica	2
The Numbers Game	5
It's a Girl!!	8
Back to School	11
What Do They Know That I Don't?	14
Yearning to Know More of the Past	17
To Save or Not to Save	20
His First Grade, and Mine	23
The Many Meanings of Friendship	26
The Wedding Pages and the Jewish Question	29
For Everything, There is a Season	32
I Am Woman, Hear Me Drain the Boiler	35
The Gender Thing	38
Good Friday	41
A Round-Trip Ticket to School	45
His Brother's Keeper	48
For Auld Lang Syne	51
Kids of the Book	54
When I'm a Mom	57
Four-stalling the Future	60
To Sleepaway Camp and Beyond	63
The Next Forty	66
It Takes a Village	69
In My Life	72

Musings on Holidays and Faith

Oh My God!	76
My Own December Dilemma	79
A Women's Room	82
The More One Tells The Story	85
The Mourning Never Stops	88

Summertime	91
A Wish for the New Year	94
Me and My *Chavrusa*	97
Fellow Travellers for the Season	100
On Passover, the Tale is in the Telling	103
Happy Birthday, Israel	106
A Jew is a Jew is a Jew	109
You Can Go Home Again	112
The Holiday Hangover	115
In Praise of Heroes	118
Passover, the Process	121
A Soccer Kicks into the New Year	124
Life in the Present Tense	127
Israel at 54: an Existential Threat	130
The Hardest Year	133
Mothers and Feminism	136
Saddam and Passover	139
My Father's Words	142
A Tale of Two Cities	145

The View from Here

For I Have Been to the Mountain Top...	149
My Own Personal Boycott	152
Reflections at a Ball Game	155
Land of Macs and Honey	158
My Own Y2K Problem	161
My Son and Joe	164
Mothers, Sons and Guns	167
A Measure of Redemption	170
Toward Redemption: a Poland Diary	173
What We Lost	178
The Glory of the Mundane	181
Rightward Bound	184
Mid-life Aliyah	187
Lessons from Cape Canaveral	190

Afterword

Come Together	194
A Matter of Time	197

Foreword
by Tova Mirvis

When I first met Rifka, she was an editor at the Jewish Telegraphic Agency and I was her intern. Sitting a few desks away, I would hear her on the phone, between articles and interviews, talking to her husband, making plans, juggling schedules. I liked watching her — here was someone who was doing it, I thought, balancing family, career, and religion. At the time, in the summer before my junior year in college, all this lay before me, somewhere in the imaginable future: jobs, husbands, children — a theoretical version of what I hoped life held in store for me.

After that summer, I ran into Rifka over the years, but our lives intersected mostly through her column as I became one of her monthly readers. In the meantime, I had gotten married and had children, and the themes and questions that were at the cornerstone of many of her columns took on new meaning for me. By reading her columns, I felt as if I still knew her, which is what the best writers do — they create a feeling of intimacy through words.

She opened a window into her home, her family, her community. Her columns are dispatches from a life unfolding and provide a rare opportunity to see what lurks behind daily life, to turn over a seemingly small moment, and in an instant, reveal the larger questions there.

Writing about motherhood, about family, about faith, and their conflicts and tensions, her voice was unwaveringly honest, wry, gentle, and reflective; she could turn a four-year-old's proposal of marriage into a meditation on Jewish education, and her experience of learning to drain the boiler into a commentary on domestic roles. As her children grew, started school, and learned to read, she captured the beauty of each moment, along with the bittersweet feeling that came with watching her children reach new stages of independence.

She captures in her essays those moments when we all wish that time would freeze. Treasuring the babyhood of her youngest child, she captures the flickering immediacy of life with small children: "With her, I wanted time to stand still. I did not want her to move into kid-dom. I wanted her to hold on to her babyhood, or toddler-hood, and all that those stages imply." Watching her son run around a chicken coop, she observes that "with him, there for that hour, there was no past, no future, only the present."

Rifka applies this same awareness of time to memories of her own parents — causing time to pause for a moment. In one of her most poignant essays, "Good Friday," she writes that "as a child what I liked best about my mother's Fridays were the pauses. In between chores, she would collapse for a few minutes in her favorite kitchen chair, sip some iced coffee and just kind of be there for the asking…. In some ways it was a prelude to Shabbat, a day devoted entirely to rest, but these moments were somehow even more precious because they were stolen out of the flurry of activity that was Friday."

These pauses surface again and again in her essays, they lift us out of the everyday, and make us look with new eyes at life around us. Writing about "The Holiday Hangover," she describes the fatigue at the end of the long string of fall holidays, but then steps back and asks, "Now that the holidays are over, we get to return to our commitments, our projects, our schedules. Somehow these words do not convey life. They convey the means to an end. They convey a constant clambering up, trying to reach some kind of plateau, some sense of accomplishment.

Maybe on the holidays, which take us out of our normal existence, we get a taste of what the plateau might feel like."

With the news of her illness, the question of time becomes more urgent, more painful. Her sense of the future altered, she describes living on "cancer time": "I can no longer peer down the road and look forward to the bar mitzvahs, the graduations, the career highlights, the new kitchen. The future now stretches about as far as next week and even that is hard to plan."

But along with the news of her illness, the chord that resonates loudest is the continuity of life, which becomes a salve for the passing of time. Whether deliberating what to pack before a move, or mourning an uncle or reconnecting with old friends or sending a child to sleep-away camp, Rifka describes the ways in which our lives are connected to our past and future. As she often did in these columns, Rifka places her moment in the context of Jewish tradition — most poignantly in a column written when she was sick. There, she observed that "Pesach is very much part of the present and also the cornerstone for our futures.... We merge different aspects of time at the seder. And though my illness has changed my perspective on what I can and cannot plan on, it has reaffirmed my faith in the longer term. For there, sitting at my seder table, will be three generations of my family, celebrating together our family's and our people's cherished traditions. And therein lies my future."

In another meditation on Jewish holidays and continuity, Rifka describes gathering her family close, hoping to be in the same spot next year. Along with the image of arms wrapping loved ones close, there is, throughout her essays, a sense of arms outstretched, not just to hold the busy-ness and unpredictability of everyday life, but also embracing just as tightly her past and her future.

Introduction
by Robert Goldblum

Managing Editor
of *The New York Jewish Week*

The newspaper columnist, unburdened by the objectivity and neutrality that govern her reporter colleagues, is a special breed of journalist. Like a favorite stool in the corner coffee shop, the columnist is, for readers, familiar, a kind of journalistic comfort zone where the rules that govern the rest of the newspaper are somehow suspended and a powerful, one-to-one connection takes place.

Great columnists take the newspaper down to the level where we all live, and with the power of their observation and the lilt of their words, they sing ballads to how extraordinary an ordinary life can be.

For readers of *The New York Jewish Week*, the country's largest Jewish newspaper and what the *Village Voice* called "the paper of record in the Jewish community," columnist Rifka Rosenwein was a singer of ballads who occupied a sacred spot in many hearts. She wrote the "Home Front" column in the paper for seven years, from 1996 until her death from cancer in the fall of 2003. She was 42.

The idea for the column was deceptively simple: Take a Jewishly committed baby boomer mom with three young kids, a thriving career as an editor in some of the country's elite business magazines, a house in the suburbs, a lawyer husband, and ageing Holocaust survivor parents, mix well, and serve monthly in the pages of the paper.

But in many ways Rifka transcended the formula. The paper wanted a strong and savvy woman's voice. More than that, we wanted someone who could translate some of the changes taking place in the Jewish community—the increasing role of women within Jewish ritual life, the changing family, the rise of Orthodox feminism, the growing focus on Jewish continuity, the fraying ties between Jews here and in Israel, the fading memory of the Holocaust—all from the front porch. Rifka accomplished that, and more.

Her front porch was in Teaneck, N.J., a heavily Modern Orthodox and tightly-knit town ten miles from Manhattan where she claimed her deep and sustaining sense of place. As her editor, I identified Rifka in the early months her column with the author line: "a writer living in Teaneck, N.J." She needled me often about this. Why did I insist on naming Teaneck? she would ask. It smacked a little too much of "vapid suburban dweller" for her tastes; it was limiting; was I making fun of her? After a while I caved and dropped the mention of Teaneck; she had developed a real following and locating her in a specific suburb didn't seem so important anymore. Neither of us could have known then how much Teaneck would come to figure in her column. For like Sherwood Anderson's Winesberg, Ohio, or Alice McDermott's Long Island, after Rifka was diagnosed with cancer in December 2001 and began to write about her illness, Teaneck became a character in her column, and in her personal drama.

It is tempting to divide Rifka's 70-odd columns into two parts: before cancer and after. We live in a confessional age where everything, *everything,* is revealed, laid bare, Oprah-ed. Yet even with that, there is a courageousness that jumps off the page in Rifka's columns about her battle with the disease.

Faced with the harsh diagnosis, she stayed true to her craft, her calling, if you will. Writers write. They do it to make sense of things, to figure out what they think, to take the measure of their experience in 800 words, and, heartbreakingly in Rifka's case, to tell her three children about their mother's life. And so, clearheadedly, at times starkly, lovingly and with theological rigor, that is what Rifka did. And that Teaneck suburb, the one she chafed against, opened its heart and reached out its arms to the writer on the front porch.

But although tempting, it would be wrong to divide Rifka's columns by that simple arithmetic — before cancer and after. For while the disease became a central part of her life, it didn't define her, either as a person or a columnist. Putting a finger on what *did* is a trickier enterprise.

Rifka was born in the summer of 1961. Her father, Zvi Rosenwein, a Polish Holocaust survivor and resistance fighter who smuggled dozens of Jews to freedom, emigrated to the United States in 1949 after being held in a German POW camp. A writer in pre-war Poland, he worked as a bedspread and drapery manufacturer in Manhattan, eventually returning to writing as a columnist for the *Algeimeiner Journal*, a noted Yiddish publication, after his retirement in 1993. Rifka's mother, Blanche, was born in Transylvania and came to America in 1925. They were married in 1958.

Rifka and her older brother, Moshe, two years her senior, grew up on the Upper West Side of Manhattan and commuted crosstown to Ramaz, the elite Modern Orthodox day school on East 85th Street. She graduated in 1979. Rifka then spent a year in Israel before enrolling in Barnard College, where she graduated Phi Beta Kappa in 1983. She continued on to Harvard's John F. Kennedy School of Government, where she received a master's degree in 1985.

Rifka's career as a journalist began at the *Wall Street Journal* in 1985, where she wrote her share of the *Journal*'s famously well-written and endearingly quirky page one "A Head" columns, the long features that begin in the center column of the front page. After two years, she was lured from the *Journal* by Steven Brill to start *Manhattan Lawyer*, a companion magazine to *American Lawyer*. After serving as editor at *American Lawyer*, Rifka became managing editor of the Jewish Telegraphic Agency, a wire service for the nation's Jewish newspapers akin to the Associated Press. Thereafter, when Steven Brill launched *Brill's Content*, a magazine devoted to aggressively covering the media, he once again reached out to Rifka. As senior writer at *Brill's Content*, Rifka reached the height of her abilities as a business and media writer. Her in-depth articles on subjects as varied as Michael Bloomberg, Fox News and the media merger frenzy, remain authoritative on their subjects and some continue to be studied at business schools across the country. When *Brill's Content* folded in 2001, Rifka became the New York editor of the Boston-based *Inc.* magazine. Then it was on to *American Demographics*, where she took over the editor's slot just three weeks before learning of her diagnosis.

Although Rifka once wrote in her diary that it was Anne Frank who inspired her to become a writer, it was her father who was perhaps the most important influence in her life. "I became a writer in no small measure because my father had been one," she writes in a "Home Front" column. It is her father's experience as a Holocaust survivor that helped shape Rifka's sensibility as a writer. Though she writes that growing up she had no recollection of being told about the Holocaust, she lived in its shadow, "with the constant sense that things were not quite right."

"Words, words, words; testimony, documents, papers — this is what my father believed in as the only way to influence opinion and preserve memory," she writes.

This is what Rifka does. She preserves the memories, bearing witness to her father's generation, and to all the Jews who didn't survive, telling and retelling and never forgetting, and finding a way to pass these memories to her kids as their *yerusha*, or inheritance. But she also bears witness to her own generation. The pain of seeing her father age, stop writing, and then stop speaking; an emotional trip back to her father's hometown in Poland, a roots journey undertaken by growing numbers of baby boomer Jews; the cruel killing fields of an Israel ripped apart by Palestinian terrorism; the shock and heartbreak of 9/11 and the fear-laden "new normal" that followed; her own battle with cancer—the arc of these columns have an unmistakable sadness, a sense of loss, of fragility, of the brokenness of things.

But there is grace here, too, and light and sweetness. And for Rifka, as always, there is the home front, for up the front lawn, through the front door, up the stairs where the three kids are, "this way lies redemption," as she puts it.

Looking back, Rifka's style, her voice, her deceptively simple wisdom, were all there in her first column, in May 1996. The central approach was there too, one she would come back to time and again: A circle radiating out from her home to the wider world, from her house to our house, linking the Jewish experience to the larger American experience. She found a way, magical when it works, to make the personal resonate beyond her particular circumstances.

The set-up for that first column was as "front porch," as you can get: "My 4-year-old son announced his first marriage proposal the other day." The catch, of course, was that Jessica, her boy's intended, wasn't Jewish. This prompted a riff on the merits of a strictly Orthodox preschool vs. her son's mixed-variety one. "The questions surrounding my 4-year-old's marriage proposal are not about intermarriage," she writes. "In short, they're about teaching my children to walk the American-Jewish walk, the tightrope act that somehow allows for remaining open to the society around us while preserving the Jewishness within us."

In her essays, more than any other theme, Rifka returns again and again to the notion of time. In a brutal irony, it is the one thing she has too little of.

She writes lyrically about time in a Jewish context, especially those long summer Shabbats that stretch languidly into nighttime. The gathering dusk brought out the poet in Rifka. "To me, the essence of Shabbat can be felt in its last few hours, particularly during the long Shabbatot of the summer months. You know that soon, within a few hours, your life will resume where you left it Friday afternoon.... But for now, as if held back by some unseen hand, you do none of this. Deliciously, you just play with the baby or ... if you're lucky, curl up with the book you never get to read."

Time and loss are forever linked for Rifka, the cancer-battling daughter of a Holocaust survivor. Her post-cancer-diagnosis columns are heartbreaking in their discussion of time. "Time seemed to me like an unbroken continuum," she wrote a few months after being diagnosed. "No more. I am now on cancer time. [It] forces you solidly into the present, and to some extent, into the past. Today is the only day I can count on."

This rupture in time is one that mirrors her parents' experience. "Both of my parents were born in Europe, to a world that no longer exists," she writes. Her mother came to America when she was a child but her parents died when she was young "and she herself was thus cut off from her own history. My father survived the Holocaust, but little else from his pre-war life survived — not his parents, not his language, not his context."

Rifka attempts to heal the rupture, trying to provide a sense of continuity between the ashes of her parents' Europe and the new dawn of Teaneck. On a summer Sunday afternoon, with her son at the plate in his Little League game, she describes the sounds in "my Modern Orthodox *shtetl*."

"Yaakov, hold the bat higher!" "Ari, keep your eye on the ball!" "Run home, Sarah, run home!" ... "And so, I thought, the transformation was complete. The great-grandchildren of the original *shtetls* in Europe, carrying the names of their murdered forebears, were running the bases in America."

As a writer, Rifka could lay her words down, like a glistening bridge across the generations, linking her parents, herself, and her kids.

In a column about a family vacation in Israel, which she so deeply loved and where she is buried, Rifka writes that when she was in the Holy Land she was reminded of the "sanctity of place" ... "Even in its modern incarnation," she writes, "Israel is the only place in the world where going to the supermarket still rises to the level of an act of faith, where taking a walk fulfills a commandment."

As Rifka battled cancer to the end, the place that was sanctified in those last days and months was Teaneck, the home front.

In the February 2002 column in which she revealed her cancer diagnosis to her readers, two months after her doctor shocked her with the news, she confides to her readers: "I left my beloved New York City for this New Jersey village eight years ago, kicking and screaming all the way about living in a close-knit, homogeneous suburb where everybody knows your business." Looking back over "every kugel lovingly brought over on a Friday afternoon; every 'emergency' sleepover that had to be arranged on a moment's notice; every prayer or Psalm said on my behalf" — in short for the outpouring of love and kindness and support from her Teaneck community — Rifka writes, "Well, all I can say is, thank God for this close-knit, homogeneous suburb where everybody knows your business."

In her last "Home Front" column, in September 2003, two months before she died, the metaphor had deepened. A lot of love was turned her way, and she was awed and humbled by it, and she felt blessed. Her life as a published writer ends with a Hebrew blessing, "the full meaning of which I have only learned these past couple of years. It's ... something you will say to another person after they have already done something wonderful. '*Tizku l'mitzvot*' — may you be worthy to perform additional positive commandments. It can truly be a '*z'chut*', a privilege, to perform an act of kindness for another. If nothing else, it means you are in a position to do so. I can think of no better wish for us all for this coming New Year." That Rosh HaShanah was Rifka's last.

The joy of seeing her eldest son gripped by the pleasure of reading — both English and Hebrew — was fodder for a column that brought Rifka's odyssey as a writer full circle. With his inheritance, his *yerusha* — a mother who has "spent my entire adult life grappling with the written word," and a grandfather who was a columnist for a Yiddish paper — it's perhaps not surprising that he announced one day that he was starting his own newspaper, "a daily 'family' newspaper, recording the annals of our family over the summer. It appears almost every morning (our subscription lapses from time to time) on the kitchen table, along with *The New York Times*.

"This newspaper is his, of course, as are the books he is reading," she writes. "I can imagine no greater satisfaction as a parent than watching as my children's imaginations take flight and their dreams begin to soar."

Robert Goldblum
New York City

Acknowledgements

I am grateful that with this book, Rifka's essays, originally appearing in *The New York Jewish Week*, are now available to a wider audience. A part of Rifka's essence and humanity lives on and for this I have many to thank.

It was Gary Rosenblatt, editor of *The New York Jewish Week*, who initially suggested that Rifka write a monthly "Home Front" column to provide a first-person narrative of American Jewish family life. Gary's strong support for Rifka's column continued throughout her seven-year tenure. After Rifka died, Gary provided invaluable support and encouragement. I am also grateful to Managing Editor Rob Goldblum for his enthusiasm and ideas and for writing a magnificent introduction. Art Director Dan Bocchino designed the evocative cover.

Tali Rosenblatt Cohen, of Laura Dail Literary Agency, first approached Rifka with the idea of publishing her essays. It was Tali who suggested dividing the book into sections along the lines they now contain. Rifka liked what she saw. "She gets it," she said. After Rifka's death, Tali, always generous, open and wise, helped navigate through the publishing world until we landed in the safe harbor of Ben Yehuda Press.

Larry Yudelson worked with Rifka at the Jewish Telegraphic Agency during her tenure as managing editor. Larry understood and supported my compulsion to reintroduce Rifka's essays in book form. At Ben Yehuda Press, Larry, together with Eve Yudelson, provided welcome advice and brought our wish to fruition.

Special thanks to Tova Mirvis for contributing an intimate and moving introduction.

Rifka's myriad friends, family and admirers were a Greek chorus encouraging this project.

Our children, Akiva, Meir and Miriam, were Rifka's muse and the focus of many, if not most, of her essays. Rifka would surely have dedicated this book to them and I can do no less.

Finally, Sandee Brawarsky provided gentle guidance and unwavering support in bringing this book, and me, to life.

Barry Lichtenberg
New York, New York
July 24, 2007

The Home Front

On Marrying Jessica

May 1996

My four-year-old son announced his first marriage proposal the other day. The announcement came while he was getting into pajamas and telling me, as he often does, about his day at school.

His class had been treated to a movie version of a book they had been reading together, *Jack and the Beanstalk*.

"And do you know who sat next to me?" he asked, in a tone of voice previously reserved for describing particularly awesome trucks.

It was Jessica who had graced the seat next to him, and my son, seemingly overcome by the magnitude of the event, promptly declared his love for Jessica and asked her to marry him. She, apparently, had accepted.

Yes, he's four, but this was still a milestone in his and my life. What did he know about marriage? Since when did he even notice girls?

Like any mother, my heart fluttered as he told me about his intended. All the usual questions raced through my head: What was she like? What kind of family was she from? Would we be able to have lunch together and really talk? Would she leave any room in his life for me?

Luckily, my son's circle of acquaintances being somewhat limited at this age, I already knew a lot about Jessica. She is a classmate of his in nursery school, she throws a great birthday party and, I must admit, she is quite cute. She's also not Jewish.

Now, don't get me wrong. I am a concerned Jewish parent, but intermarriage is not exactly at the top of my parental worries right now. I am much more focused on toilet-training my two-year-old.

But the episode with Jessica jarred me, nonetheless, and turned my thinking to more immediate issues.

My children attend a preschool that, while under Jewish auspices, welcomes students from all different backgrounds. A large number of intermarried couples seem to have found the program a particularly good fit.

My husband and I chose it mostly because we thought it was the best preschool we saw — and because it was close enough to our house that I wouldn't have to worry about carpooling.

But we considered it an added benefit that as an outgrowth of attending the school, our children, and our family as a whole, would meet and socialize with Jews of all stripes, and non-Jews, as well. As Modern Orthodox Jews, we also thought the choice would allow us the flexibility to introduce our kids to the rituals and traditions of our more stringent brand of religion at our own pace, rather than at one dictated by an Orthodox preschool.

We planned all along to send our kids to a Jewish day school as soon as they reach kindergarten, so what harm could there be in sending them to a less sheltered preschool?

After three years in the school, I remain convinced that there is no harm, but I also realize that my question can be, and is being asked by Jewish parents at every stage in their children's education.

In fact, most of the parents that I have met at my son's preschool are not sending their children to a Jewish day school for many of the same reasons that I do not send my children to an exclusively Jewish preschool: They want to expose their children to a broader spectrum of backgrounds, and they want to practice their Judaism the way they see fit.

As one parent put it to me, "Jewish day schools are not reality. The reality is that most people my son will come in contact with are not Jewish, so why should I try to protect him from that?"

Some parents will make the same argument at high school; others will draw the line at college. By that time, of course, the decision is no longer just the parents'. But at each point the challenge remains the same: How do you prepare your kids for the "real world" — which for most American Jews is not an exclusively Jewish one — while at the same time preserving their identity as Jews?

The questions surrounding my four-year-old's marriage proposal are not about intermarriage. They are about what to do when he has a playdate with a friend who doesn't have a kosher home. They're about being asked why his best buddy Kevin gets both a Christmas tree and a Chanukah menorah, while he only gets a menorah. They're about being invited to a birthday party on Tisha B'Av.

In short, they're about teaching my children to walk the American Jewish walk, the tightrope act that somehow allows for remaining open to the society around us while preserving the Jewishness within us. It's one thing for the community at large to be asking the big questions about "continuity"; it's another thing to put matzah in your kid's lunchbox during Passover, knowing full well that most of the other children will be having their regular peanut butter sandwiches. Judaism — and parenting — are in the details.

As for my son's betrothal, my concerns have abated somewhat. The engagement was short-lived. Apparently, Jessica has decided that she doesn't play with boys anymore. And my son has returned to his trucks, at least for now.

The Numbers Game

July 1996

As anyone who has ever been pregnant in New York will tell you, walking around the city with a large belly is an open invitation for complete strangers to come right up to you and share their thoughts about your condition.

The commentators fall into several categories.

There are the prognosticators, as in, "It's definitely a boy. I can tell by the way you're carrying." This is often followed, a block later, by another stranger insisting that you're having a girl, based, of course, on the way you're carrying.

There are the advice-dispensers, who, when you're already at the salad bar, feel compelled nonetheless to quote *What to Expect When You're Expecting*, chapter and verse, on the benefits of a healthy diet during pregnancy.

And my personal favorite: the sizer-uppers, as in, "Wow! Are you HUGE! Are you having twins or something?" This exclamation is particularly endearing when it is made by a man sitting down on the subway, staring straight at that "HUGE" belly, while you are struggling to keep your balance holding onto the rail above him.

But the only comment that has ever given me pause comes from what I might call the number-crunchers. This reaction can be volunteered only when I am in the company of my two children. And it can be summed up best by the woman who passed me on the street, pushing my younger son in a stroller while the older one walked beside me: "You're having another one?!"

Yes, I am. (Or rather, I should say, "we are," since my husband always mumbles something about "we're in this together" as I stumble to the bathroom at 4 a.m.)

In my office and in America at large, three seems a bit excessive, though by no means unheard of. In my own Modern Orthodox Jewish community, three doesn't raise an eyebrow and four is quite common. And, of course, in some Jewish circles, three doesn't even cut it as a bare minimum.

But the "numbers" comment gives me pause because my husband and I took this step with no small amount of trepidation — and not least because the thought of having more children than adults in the house terrifies us.

We both come from homes of two children each. Our parents, all born in Europe, survived tragic circumstances, struggled to find their place in a new land, married late, and devoted their middle age to raising their children. Two children for them seemed like more than they could have ever hoped for.

My husband and I, like many of our generation who are able, are having more children than our parents did. There are many reasons for this, and many reasons that are unique to each family. I don't think this is purely a religious phenomenon, motivated by halachic principles.

Part of it is simply that we are able; we are better prepared materially and emotionally for more kids. But I think, also, that there is somewhat of a tribal thing going on. Many of us seem caught up in an almost feverish effort to replenish the much-depleted Jewish population. It is, in part, a numerical effort, aimed simply at increasing the size of our people, making up for all the children who never got the chance to grow into parents, all the families that never were.

But the replenishing represents more than just numbers. There is, in this increased birthrate, an effort — however quixotic — at permanence. Somehow, we feel, the more children we have, the more protected, the less vulnerable we are. We can leave behind more Jews than there were when we came into the world. There seems to us a real strength in numbers.

Of course, sheer numbers did not shield our grandparents in Europe. For national permanence, we look to the modern State of Israel and our own political strength in the United States to protect us and keep us whole.

But in our own lives and the lives of our individual communities, we can look only to our children to guarantee a future.

Each child is precious, and in each child a universe of possibilities resounds. As parents, we invest in each one all our resources and all our love. In fact, after I had my first, I was convinced that there was no need to have another — my son alone could keep me occupied and preoccupied for a lifetime.

But we had another, at least in part because we didn't want our eldest to be alone. And we, as a community, seem to want to have the second or the third or the fourth, so that we too won't be alone.

In my world growing up, the Jews seemed so very much alone, so depleted. My nuclear family was small; my extended family virtually eliminated by the Holocaust, the Jewish people abandoned during the war and then struggling in the Middle East against a hostile world.

I never want my children to feel that way. I want them to feel that being Jewish is a growing, vibrant enterprise, that they are part of a greater whole.

In some ways, my peers and I are trying to make up for what was lost in the past. But at the same time, we are trying to build a future for the Jewish people, child by child by child.

It's a Girl!!

October 1996

And so now I have a daughter. Every woman I meet smiles knowingly when they learn I have had a girl. Women I barely know have approached me with my little pink bundle, and as if we were cohorts in some quiet conspiracy, whispered to me, "There is nothing like having a daughter."

Mind you, I have two sons whom I love dearly. And despite all the excitement generated by having a girl, I have discovered that at the grand old age of two months, the two genders act remarkably alike. My daughter cries much like her brothers did, keeps me up at night much like her brothers did, and melts away all the frustrations of infancy with her newfound smile, much like her brothers did.

Okay, granted, her clothes are cuter. But I don't think that's what all these women were referring to. The concept of "daughterhood" is fraught with associations for most women. After all, every woman's primordial identity is as a daughter. I suppose it is the same way for men when they have a son. Having a child of your own gender is perhaps the ultimate act of re-creation; it is as close as any of us will ever get to immortality.

But I think for a woman, especially a Jewish woman, having a daughter means something more. Jewish women carry with them a unique heritage — that of sustaining the very foundation of Jewish life, the Jewish family, throughout the generations. I and most other Jewish women hope to bequeath to their daughters at least some of the accumulated wisdom of their foremothers, be it a secret recipe or a particular way of coping with the trials and travails of family life.

At the same time, many Jewish women facing the modern world —with all its bewildering choices and trade-offs — relish the opportunity to take part in helping a new generation of women fashion new roles for themselves and resolve some of the issues that have bedeviled those who came before them. I don't think the tensions inherent in being a modern Jewish woman will ever disappear, but I can hope that my daughter will somehow find a better way.

But I discovered early on that it will be no mean feat to pass on to my daughter her rich Jewish heritage while at the same time prepare her for a brave new world.

After my daughter was born, I looked, as I usually do, to Jewish tradition to help me express my joy, my hopes, and my thanks to God for bringing me this healthy baby. But, as my husband put it, when it comes to celebrating the birth of a girl, traditional Judaism is ritually challenged.

There is no ancient ritual, handed down from generation to generation, to welcome this latest addition into the fold of the Jewish people. As difficult as a *brit milah* can be for new parents (not to mention the baby), they can take comfort in the fact that this ceremony has been performed for thousands of years and truly signals the arrival of a new Jewish life, filled with promise and joy.

It is this strong sense of tradition that imparts meaning and legitimacy to the event. The ritual also helps shape and focus the feelings of the celebrants. During the first week after each of my sons was born, I was, like any new mother, a complete wreck. It is definitely not an easy time to plan a party for your 70 closest friends and relatives. But when the day arrived, I had a script I could follow — that everyone there was familiar with — to help me and those closest to me mark this most emotional of occasions.

It is this way after, God forbid, a loved one passes away and the rituals of *shiva* and mourning set in. Judaism gives us blessings and rituals and prayers to help us cope, to help us celebrate, to help us express our emotions, to help us infuse meaning into the events that mark our lives. And by reciting the same words said by our fellow Jews around the world and for thousands of years, we bring these events into larger focus and make out of individual joy or sorrow a communal joy or sorrow, as well.

And so, after our daughter was born, my husband and I at first felt lost. We felt abandoned by our tradition. But then we started asking around. Others we knew had crafted their own *simchat bat* ceremonies, but this was still largely uncharted territory. Suddenly, we were given an opportunity to create something new — but not out of whole cloth. We ended up digging deeper into our tradition than we might have for a ceremony already prescribed.

We went back to the sources, learning Jewish law as it pertained to the birth of a girl. We looked up Psalms and other texts that seemed appropriate for the occasion. We consulted with friends, colleagues, rabbis, teachers. It really took a village to put our *simchat bat* together.

But in the end, when 70 of our closest friends and relatives showed up to help us celebrate the birth of our daughter, the event felt highly personal, and at the same time, very much part of a larger whole. It felt, in fact, something like a Jewish ritual.

Perhaps, by the time my daughter has a daughter of her own, this kind of ceremony may actually feel like home.

Back to School

September 1997

Math was my least favorite subject in school. I didn't enjoy it, I wasn't particularly good at it, and to top it off, my older brother was a veritable math genius who made all my efforts in that direction seem rather lame.

So imagine my trepidation when, upon entering the sacred halls of junior high school, I was told that the math teacher I was to have that year was the most feared teacher in the entire school.

I will never forget the first day of his class. In most of the other classes, we were allowed to choose our own seats. Not in Mr. Goetz's class. He lined us up at the back of the room in size order and seated the shortest kids up front. Needless to say, I was among the shortest in my class and was placed in perhaps the most undesirable seat in the entire room: right in front of the teacher.

Other teachers assumed we would take notes in our notebooks however we saw fit. Not in Mr. Goetz's class. He told us exactly how to take notes, exactly which supplies we would need each day in class, and exactly how to place the textbook on the desk in front of us. I can't even describe the intricacies of how we were supposed to prepare our homework.

The final warning he left us with: Whatever you do, never, ever be late to class. As soon as the bell would ring, he would lock the door to the room. And you could just march yourself over to the principal's office for the duration of the period. By this point, I knew I was doomed. I perennially overslept, was constantly late for school — and Mr. Goetz was the first class of the day!

That night at home, I was hysterical. The first day of seventh grade in a yeshiva junior high — with ten new subjects and ten new teachers — might seem overwhelming to a young student. But I had had no trouble pinpointing the man who was clearly out to make my life miserable: Mr. Goetz. Somehow, I knew that he was going to loom over my entire junior high and high school career.

And so he did. And so he still does. This past summer, I attended his wedding. He was at mine nearly a decade ago. From time to time, he's invited me to speak at my old high school — where he not too long ago celebrated his 25th year of teaching (in my alma mater, the junior high and high school were connected and shared the same faculty).

I never did get good at math, and dropped it as an object of study immediately after graduating from high school. But Mr. Goetz was one of those rare teachers whose teachings went far beyond the subject matter at hand.

His tough stance on work habits, which terrified me at first, taught me a sense of discipline that I bring to my work to this day. And if you worked hard, and still didn't get it, he spent hours of his own time helping you. While I sometimes yearned to just be told how to do a math problem, he never taught any subject without fully explaining the underlying concept. He made you sweat, but he forced you to think. And perhaps most importantly, he never took fear or lack of smarts as an excuse. As corny as it may sound, he taught me to believe in myself.

He also proved a friend and a mentor outside the classroom. He was an avid bird watcher, a fanatical tennis player, and a dogged urban cyclist. From this I learned to pursue whatever iconoclastic interests I might have, no matter how far removed from my professional career.

My math teacher's original love, ironically, was English, and he served as our high school yearbook adviser. When, five years after I first walked into his class, he plucked me from obscurity to become the yearbook editor — a position I had not even put myself in the running for — he opened up a world to me from which, as you can see, I have never departed.

In this season of school beginnings, with the freshness of new notebooks and the tentativeness of new class assignments in the air, I can feel blessed that I had a teacher like Mr. Goetz, and a school that cultivated a whole cadre of inspired and inspiring teachers. In Judaism, of course, there is no higher calling.

I can only hope that my children will each, in their own turn, be fortunate enough to have a Mr. Goetz in their lives.

Don't think, by the way, that the terror ever completely dissipated. I now know my former math teacher for the warm, funny, loyal man that he is. But I have never called him anything but Mr. Goetz.

What Do They Know That I Don't?

December 1997

I suffer from a preoccupation — no, I'd say an obsession — with the lives of other women.

Every day, I look through the newspaper scanning for any article having to do with the juggling act that defines womanhood today. Every magazine that I subscribe to, I turn first to the table of contents to see if there are any stories about women/workplace/family. And, whatever I read or see, I know that as an observant Jew, I have to add one more ingredient to this complicated stew: my religious commitments.

I am an equal opportunity student of other women. I devour stories on successful businesswomen who manage to attend their kids' soccer games on Saturday. I read and re-read countless articles about one of the top female executives at PepsiCo giving it all up to spend more time with her kids.

At the same time, I pore over articles about the working poor, women who have to drop their kids off at substandard day care in order to get to their $5.25-an-hour jobs, women who don't have the luxury of making choices.

I go to visit a friend out of state and I spend the entire evening watching her nightly routine with her three kids, observing like a scientist, making mental notes for improvement in my own schedule.

I have lunch with an old college roommate whom I haven't seen in ages. She has six children now, plus a career in academia. I spend the entire lunch peppering her with questions: When do you have time for each kid? When do you have time for your research? How do you divide your day? Your week? And, above all, when do you have time to make dinner?

On these long winter Saturday nights, when Shabbat is over early and I am fairly well rested, I always promise myself, "tonight is the night I'm going to finally do..." fill in the blank.

And when, instead, my husband and I end up in front of the VCR with take-out Chinese food, I often think to myself, I bet this accomplished woman is not renting a mindless movie tonight. She is probably deep in the middle of the third chapter of her next scholarly treatise. Another friend is probably preparing art projects for her kids for the next day.

Is that the answer? Too many rented movies? Is that why I'm not accomplishing all that I set out to do? Is that why my life seems like I just lurch from situation to situation, constantly pulled in all different directions, rather than follow a clear path that would lead to fulfillment and satisfaction?

Maybe it's the reporter in me. What exactly do I expect to find by reading about all these other women or interviewing peers and colleagues about how they manage their juggling act? I know that everyone's exact circumstances are different and I certainly know there's no magic formula.

But I realize that I am not really looking for answers. I am firmly convinced that there is no one right answer, no one correct way to lead a life that includes family, work, community, and self. And that is part of the conundrum.

Those of us with the luxury of choice have so very many choices. And each one of those choices is fraught with profound value. There is a sense I have that I am playing a zero-sum game; that is, that for everything I choose to do in one sphere of my life, there is a loss recorded in another.

If I choose to spend an hour in my kid's school, that is an hour I have spent not working, not making money and advancing my hard-earned career. And if I choose to spend an hour at work, that is an hour not spent with my children, not enriching their lives and my own, not nurturing my family. And if I take an hour to buy winter boots for the kids and get groceries for the house, that is an hour not spent catching up with my husband or reaching out to a friend.

Every choice I make, it seems, involves a trade-off. And every choice reflects not just the situation of the moment, but a deeper system of values, of priorities, of fundamentals.

It is draining to make these decisions constantly, and to make them, largely, alone. Women of my generation have few role models to follow, few paths that have been trailblazed before us. Observant Jewish women engaged in the workplace have even fewer.

And so, I look to my peers and to articles about my peers not for solutions, but for a sense of community. I look for alternatives, I look to see how other women made their choices and whether their decision-making bears on my own. I look for a sense that I am not alone in this, that others face this dizzying array of choices every day and that others make compromises too.

And I look so that maybe, one day, my daughter will have an easier time of it.

Yearning to Know More of the Past

June 1998

Recently I came across some old pictures of my parents. "Old" is not really the right word; these are pictures taken of them when they were young, before they were married, before they had kids.

There is my mother, smartly dressed, posing with her sister and cousin outside their apartment building; there is my father, open collar but with the ever-present suit, striding along some European boulevard, eyes staring off in the distance. They are the same, and yet not the same, as they are today, or as I remember them from my childhood years.

Like most children, even adult children, I never think of my parents as having had a life before I was born. I could never conceive of them as anything other than my parents, whose sole purpose on this Earth was to raise me, and I guess my brother, too.

It is difficult to envision my parents as real people, much like myself, for whom raising children was just one of many aspects of their lives. It is hard to remember that they lived full, rich, often dramatic lives before I was ever that proverbial twinkle in their eyes. And even after my brother and I were born, they no doubt continued to have interests and conflicts and triumphs and defeats — a whole inner life — that had little or nothing to do with their children.

I suppose one day my own children will think of me in much the same one-dimensional manner. But at least they will have the advantage of being quite familiar with the world in which I grew up and in which I spent my early adult years before they were born. I have no such access to the early lives of my parents.

My children were born in the same country as I was — in the very same hospital, in fact; they speak the same language that I did as a child; their schooling is very similar to mine; their middle-class, observant Jewish lifestyle is similar to the one in which I was raised. And now, as they reach the age when they are getting curious about my own childhood, they actually have my parents to ask questions of and my childhood home, intact, to visit.

My children's lives, in short, are a continuum of mine, in ways that mine never was vis-a-vis my parents'. Both my parents were born in Europe, to a world that no longer exists. My mother came to America when she was a child, but her parents died when she was young and she herself was thus cut off from her own history. My father survived the Holocaust, but little else from his pre-war life survived — not his parents, not his language, not his context.

In my parents' lives, there is no continuum. There is, instead, a dramatic break, a rupture that no photographs or memories can ever truly repair. Each of them, in early adulthood, had to reinvent themselves.

And I, as their daughter, have been trying to reinvent them, as well. For in reimagining my parents' lives, I am trying to connect with my own past; I am attempting to create a continuum. My parents are not ones to talk freely of their early experiences, and I, like so many of my generation, am left with only the shrapnel of their shattered lives. I know one anecdote here, one snippet there. Every so often, particularly now, as my children get older and more inquisitive, I am struck by how bereft this absence of a family past has left me.

As soon as I began reading "Where She Came From," by Helen Epstein — a journalist, scholar, and child of survivors — I knew I was not alone. Ms. Epstein spent more than six years retracing the lives of the great-grandmother and grandmother she never knew, and that of her mother, whom she realized she only partly knew. The effort alone speaks volumes; this yearning to connect the dots of our past runs very deep.

"To be rooted is perhaps the most important and least recognized need of the human soul," Ms. Epstein quotes Simone Weil as saying. "To be able to give, one has to possess; and we possess no other life, no other living sap, than the treasures stored up from the past and digested, assimilated and created afresh by us."

To Save or Not to Save

August 1998

What is the statute of limitations for letters from camp — my own, not my children's? How about for teen-age diaries? Trinkets salvaged from a trip to Europe as a young adult?

How long can these things be saved, tucked away in a drawer or box, hidden from view, rarely taken out?

These are some of the more arcane questions I am faced with as my family and I prepare to move into a new home. As anyone who has ever moved can attest, it is a traumatic experience. And the older you are and the more memories you've accumulated in one place, the harder it is to uproot yourself.

And so, in some ways, the process of packing becomes a process of trying to decide what memories to take with you. And that boils down basically to sorting through your stuff.

"Stuff" is the technical term for things that somehow make their way into your home, mostly when you're not looking. Once they're there, you can't quite figure out what to do with them. So you save them. For what, you're not quite sure. For the kids? The grandkids? The would-be biographer coming to chronicle your life well after you're gone?

I'm not talking here about the obvious items, things you know you're going to keep, or at least things I know I'm going to keep: the kids' first pairs of shoes; my high school yearbook; the card that came with the first bouquet of flowers my husband ever gave me.

And I'm also not talking about the things that, however reluctantly, you know it's time to part with: The out-of-date, chewed-up guidebook for London that we used on our family vacation; the collection of Broadway Playbills that I kept going for a while in the mid-1980s; the plastic blue baby bath that I used when the kids were infants.

No, it's the material in between that challenges me most. This is the true definition of "stuff": The correspondence between me and my best friend when I was in Israel for a year and she had already started college back in New York; the response cards sent in by family and friends to the invitation to our wedding; and, of course, the toughest one of all — the kids' endless collection of school and camp projects that are each precious when brought home that day by an excited child, but quickly start to look redundant when put into one collective storage box.

How to decide what to save and what to toss? In our noble attempt not to move junk to our new house, my husband has instituted a rather ruthless standard: If we haven't used it for more than one year, it's out. Well, that's fine for old clothes or even old toys. But the same rule can't apply for old photographs or old letters or old records (those things that made music before the CD was invented).

Clearly, these are not items that we "use" in any sense of the word. They are there to remind us of who we are, or, perhaps, who we used to be. A souvenir from a trip taken many years ago reminds us not only of that adventure, but also of what was important to us then, what we took the time to gaze at and admire, what we made the effort to save.

My own life and my profession are very caught up with words, so perhaps more than most people, I tend to save the written word — letters, cards, even notes scribbled during class in high school. Each one of us tends to save the tokens of a time that meant the most to us then, and often, what still means the most to us.

As I sit in my attic late at night, pretending to pack but actually just going through my stuff, I am amazed at some of the continuity in my life and saddened all over again by those connections that I have lost over the years. I try to apply my husband's utilitarian standard, and find, over and over again, that it just doesn't work. And I realize that, ultimately, what I save is not for my grandchildren, or even for posterity. It is my stuff and I'm saving it for me. It's true, I don't take it out very often, and most of it serves no real purpose, but it is part of who I am and I would be the poorer without it.

And so I'm taking a lot of my stuff with me, to my husband's chagrin. Moving is a logistical nightmare, but getting ready to move, I have learned, can be an emotionally cathartic experience. I have purged myself of whatever it is that I have finally decided is junk and I have gotten a new appreciation of the things that, for whatever reason, I've decided, once again, to hold onto. In keeping this stuff, I have reclaimed parts of my past, and of myself. And I'm taking it with me to help make my new house into my home.

His First Grade, and Mine

October 1998

Well, the pencils have been sharpened, the notebooks labelled and the folders divided by subject. Old clothes have been tried on, new clothes purchased, and hair has been put to the scissors. A big wooden desk has even been added to the bedroom.

I am finally ready for first grade... I mean, my son is. It was when I came home from orientation all excited because of who was going to be in my class that my husband felt compelled to sit me down and explain to me carefully that it was not "my" class, not "my" first grade, and not "my" homework to worry about.

Okay, so he's my eldest. And yes, I was one of those geeks who actually really liked school as a kid. But in first grade, who didn't? It was all so exciting, so grown-up, so responsible. The beginning of the school year brought with it such a sense of freshness and opportunity. Opening up a brand new, squeaky clean notebook, putting on that first new sweater of the season, figuring out which friends were in your class — these are powerful, almost palpable memories that return to me every autumn.

But this fall, of course, was special. My eldest child had caught up with my own memories. Finally, after years of traveling through the wasteland of jobs and adulthood, school has re-entered my life. And I welcome it, perhaps too enthusiastically. I welcome the learning, I welcome the friendships, I welcome the rituals and rhythms of the school year.

As a friend of mine remarked recently, I now have a child who has reached an age that I can remember from my own youth. As accomplished as I might feel as a parent when my child takes his first steps or completes his first sentence, I myself have no memories of reaching these milestones.

But first grade — I remember my teachers' names, where I sat, who I sat next to. I remember a low point, when the Hebrew teacher picked up a girl in my class and told her she was her best girl. And I remember a high point, when I wrote my first story, about a cat and a mouse. I remember some of the friends I made —one of whom remains my friend to this day. And I remember feeling hurt and left out when some old friends from kindergarten didn't include me in their new clique.

Do I wish for my son any of those hurtful experiences? Of course not. Do I know they will come nonetheless? Probably. What I wish for him is the richness and depth that a great education and a stimulating school environment can give him. What I wish for him are the kinds of friends who may last into adulthood, and all the joy — and occasional pain — those friendships can bring.

I look around at his school, at his class, at his teachers and at his friends, and I see the potential for such wishes to be fulfilled. And that's what gets me excited all over again. Perhaps there is the element of wanting to relive my own youth. But really, I'm quite content not to be six anymore. It is his first grade now, not mine. And I will just have to learn to restrain myself when those first homework assignments come in.

But still, with a few years of experience over him, I know how many doors first grade is going to open for my son. Already, I see how reading has not only opened books for him, but street signs and newspapers and letters arriving in the mail. Everywhere he looks is something new to read, or to count or even to recite in Hebrew.

And I see the friendships he is forming, the shared interests he and his buddies are cultivating (mostly in the Yankees), even the fights he has and the way he has learned to make up afterwards.

His childhood, and his memories of his childhood, are beginning in earnest. And first grade will always remain that starting point. I am nervous for him, excited for him, fearful for him, happy for him. At the same time, I recognize that not doing his homework for him is only the first of many hurdles that I will not be able to overcome for him. My education is continuing, after all.

The Many Meanings of Friendship

November 1998

I recently attended the wedding of a good friend. There are few events that I enjoy more than this, and the older my friends and I have gotten, the more joyous the celebrations have become.

This particular friend was one of a loosely defined circle that I fell into when I first moved back to New York after graduate school. We were all single, in our mid-to-late 20s or early 30s, living on the West Side, religiously observant while at the same time ambitious in our professional careers. We were drawn to each other by our shared interests — the No. 1, of course, being: getting married.

While we chased that primary, seemingly elusive, goal, we allowed ourselves a few distractions along the way. We went to the movies, swapped books, and traveled together. We formed a kind of informal support network. We took each other out to dinner when nobody else would; we made Shabbat meals together so that we would seldom have to eat by ourselves; we went with each other to singles events so we would never have to leave alone; we called each other at all hours of the day and night, so the phone would not seem so silent.

We spent countless hours, particularly late at night, talking and talking and talking, and laughing, and even crying. Yes, of course we would get off our chest a description of the latest disaster date we'd been on, but often, the conversation would veer off into discussions about ourselves that were quite illuminating (we had the luxury then to be totally self-absorbed).

Sometimes we were too caught up in the man of the hour to appreciate fully what we had in each other. We had companionship, we had support, we had deep, abiding friendship.

As I look back on it now, it was not only that these friendships sustained us through a difficult time in our lives; these friendships helped define us, helped us understand ourselves better, helped us learn how to love and how to share. They were, in many ways, wonderful stepping stones to the kind of relationship that marriage entails. Consciously or not, we managed to weave some pretty tight bonds that hold many of us together still.

And that is why it was such a pleasure to see each other at this friend's wedding. We were reminded not only of how far we have come, but also of how much we have shared. It was a joy to look around at the wedding and see most of my circle married now, many engaged in raising families and still pursuing professional goals. We all seem, on some level, to have "settled down," but we know better about each other — beneath that seemingly conventional, suburban mom lies the intelligent, complex, sensitive person that we came to know years ago.

Not that there's anything wrong with being a conventional, suburban mom. I'm actually kind of enjoying the role right now. But that's because I've been very fortunate, as have many of my friends. This friend's wedding came on the eve of my own 10th wedding anniversary, which, of course, is a good time to reflect on the institution of marriage. (No, this column is not just a elaborate ploy to remind my husband of our upcoming anniversary. It's on the 24th, dear.)

My husband takes a lot of ribbing in this space, but the time has come to 'fess up. Behind every loud-mouthed feminist such as myself — especially one who chooses to share her life story with the public once a month — lies a very patient and supportive husband. My husband has allowed me the comforts and security of being a conventional, suburban mom while giving me the freedom and flexibility to pursue my own quirky dreams.

It's more than just passive support. He leads by example. He works hard, but he has always put family and friends first. And if he believes in something, he does not sit idly by. On the first Shabbat after we were married, he pushed the challah tray over to my plate when it was time to say the blessing, and I've been reciting it ever since. The generosity of that single act has stayed with me always. By now, it is only one of dozens more acts of kindness — "feminist" or otherwise — always on his own initiative, always *min halev,* from the heart.

He is a wonderful, kind, loving husband and an incredible, involved, inspiring father. And besides all his other attributes, he is — all wrapped up in one — everything that I learned to value so many years ago when I was, in effect, looking for him. He is, above all, my dearest friend, and it is his friendship and love that will always sustain me.

To him, I wish a most happy anniversary. And to my newlywed friend and all those in attendance at her wedding: *nur auf simchas* — we should continue to meet only on happy occasions.

The Wedding Pages and the Jewish Question

January 2003

Step aside, gentlemen. You will have no interest in this column, I guarantee it.

Okay, girls. It's about the wedding pages. Come on, admit it, how many of you turn to those pages in the Styles section of the *Times* every Sunday morning? No matter what else is going on in the world — and these days, Lord knows, there is plenty — it is the first section I turn to every week.

Even the most well educated, sophisticated and accomplished women I know — friends and professional colleagues — read these pages religiously. Together, we can dish about some of the couples, particularly those portrayed in the "Vows" feature, as if we knew them ourselves and had just attended the wedding. "Can you believe she met him at a bar?" "What was she thinking when she picked out that hideous dress?" "They got married on a ski slope?!" To quote the mother of one of the men featured in the first gay commitment announcement, "Oy vey."

A former colleague of mine referred to the wedding pages as the "women's sports pages." The difference being, of course, that on the wedding pages, everybody is a winner.

The pages are such a draw for women, and perhaps particularly for Jewish women, that one of the ads that appears fairly regularly on the main wedding page reads as follows: "WOMEN (in large, bold print). Are you feeling overwhelmed, under appreciated and unfulfilled? Is your personal relationship less than you would like it to be?" And so on. "If the answer is YES to any one of these questions, then the Kabbalah for Women course at the Kabbalah Centre of New York is for you!"

Clearly, stressed out, neurotic, and mystically-challenged women constitute the wedding pages' target audience.

In an effort at full disclosure, I will admit that I placed my own wedding announcement in the *Times*. But I got married at a time when the *Times*' wedding announcements were a much more low-key affair. There was no Styles section, nor a designated spot where you could find the announcements each week. I got married on Thanksgiving, which of course was a Thursday, and so my announcement ran the next day, in an obscure part of the Metro section where no one except me and my parents could find it. Why did I do it? What can I say? I'm a journalist; I've always wanted to make it into *The New York Times*.

But there's no way I'd make the cut today. First of all, I don't have a glamorous enough picture, nor the right kind of pedigree to go with it. And besides, I met my husband on a blind date. What kind of a story would that make?

So what is it exactly that attracts me to these announcements? It's not as if I actually know any of these people, although once in a while I'll recognize the name of a former colleague or classmate. Most of the time, the people on the pages are so ridiculously wealthy or overly educated or their ancestors came over on the Mayflower, that there's no way I would ever cross paths with any of them.

Sure, there's the element of sheer voyeurism. It's a glimpse into the lives of the rich and not-so-famous at one of their happiest moments. It's also like reading a series of romantic 19th-century novels in miniature — as in Jane Austen, where the entire point of a woman's existence is to get married, and to marry well, and where everything always ends up happily ever after. Or so it would seem. At least Jane Austen had a sense of irony.

As I get older, I find myself reading the wedding pages much the way my mother does. I look for the Jews. Yes, my eye goes straight to the Jewish names in the headlines. Then I look to see if it's two Jews marrying each other. Then I look to see if a rabbi is officiating. I quietly bemoan every mixed marriage, and every ceremony that a priest conducts with a rabbi "participating," or vice versa. Every week I get a thumbnail version of the unbridled assimilation of American Jewry, especially among the upper echelons of society, and it is sobering.

So with all the allure and sociological information that can be gleaned from the wedding pages, why is it a universally acknowledged truth that only women read them? Too much romance? Not enough competition? My husband has a different theory. Men avoid these pages for the precise reason that women read them. "It reminds us of our own wedding day," says my husband, in one of his more endearing moments.

So, my fellow females, keep enjoying the wedding pages, and all the other *narishkeit*, or nonsense, that fills the Styles section. In a time of impending war, a lousy economy, and the constant threat of terrorism, what's wrong with a little escapism? So break a glass, drink a *l'chaim*, and let's pray for a time when who's marrying whom really is all we have to worry about.

For Everything, There is a Season

September 1998

Until this past summer, I had been blessed with never having lost a member of my family. But in July, my uncle passed away. He was married to my mother's sister for 52 years and our families have always been close. My uncle had been in declining health in recent years, but the end came swiftly and suddenly. Nobody was prepared.

Still, his death was not tragic like that of a person cut down in his youth. He had lived a long, happy, fulfilling life. When he died, his wife, children, and grandchildren were nearby, just where he liked them. His funeral, which brought together my mother's entire extended family, was naturally sad. But it was also a celebration of his life and a reminder of how satisfying that life had been for him.

While I mourned my uncle, I couldn't help but look around at his funeral and reflect on my family, in its broadest terms. Family, after all, was the single most important driving force in my uncle's life and it was a tribute to him and my aunt that people came from near and far to pay their respects.

He was the first of my mother's generation to pass away in our family; I couldn't help thinking that his death marked the end of a chapter in our lives. As we walked through the cemetery to his grave site, there were the members of my generation escorting their now elderly parents, holding them tight, the way the parents once held the children. The younger grandchildren were not present, of course, but those who are teen-agers and young adults walked on their own, unattended, unencumbered.

I had the sense that a torch was being passed. My grandparents died before any of my generation was born; in fact, they did not even live to see my mother and her siblings married. My uncle was the family patriarch on my mother's side. He and my aunt were married first; their children, now hovering around 50, were the first born in my mother's family. It was their house that we went to for all the holidays and family gatherings, and my uncle, with his domineering personality, was always master of ceremonies.

With his passing, I felt the power and the energy and the leadership of my parents' generation beginning to ebb. Or had it done so years ago and I hadn't noticed? It has been me and my brother and my cousins making the Pesach seders and the Thanksgiving dinners and the Chanukah parties for several years already. It is us worrying now about the tuition bills and the jobs and the state of the economy. As my husband and I joke all the time, it is our parents who now have the time and luxury to concern themselves with little things like world peace and the general decline of civilization.

This stage in my family's life, while poignant, is a natural one. The slow and deliberate transfer from one generation to the next is a much better alternative than the one that befell my parents and their peers. My mother's parents' untimely deaths and my father's parents' murders in the Holocaust left my parents bereft of an older, wiser generation from whom to gain sustenance and guidance. My generation has been more fortunate and my children's even more so — they have not only their parents, but also their grandparents to learn from.

This, after all, is the essence of the Jewish family: to pass along from one generation to the next all that has come before. The richness and depth of our heritage is our children's *"yerushah,"* their greatest inheritance, and the building blocks of our future.

And so, as we approach this most holy and thoughtful and soul-searching time of year, I mourn for my uncle and I pray that others of his generation are not soon to follow. But I am also grateful to have had him in my life for as long as I did, and even more grateful to have my parents still beside me.

As I do every Rosh HaShanah, I will gather my family tight around me in shul, at home and in my prayers. And I will thank God that there are ties that bind us very dose, *m'dor l'dor* — from generation to generation. And I will pray to have my family just as close next year, with that much more to have passed between us.

L'Shanah Tova Tikatayvu V'Techataymu.

I Am Woman, Hear Me Drain the Boiler

August 1997

This week, I got empowered.

Some Jewish women get empowered by going to feminism conferences; others from attending a moving ritual performed, perhaps for the first time, by a woman; still others are moved to act after reading a powerful text that somehow "speaks" to them.

Me, I got empowered by the Public Service Electric & Gas Company.

It went something like this. It was about 96 degrees outside, and my husband, bless his worried soul, decided it was high time to have our boiler inspected. Besides, we were entitled to a free inspection by the gas company every 10 years, and time was running out.

My husband takes great pride in the upkeep of our home and is, admittedly, quite handy around our suburban New Jersey house. I, on the other hand, grew up in a Manhattan apartment and know nothing about home maintenance.

In a clear case of reverse sexism, I have chosen to remain completely ignorant on the subject, and have relegated all household chores to my husband's domain.

But, of course, since I work at home and my husband is busy all day at a "real" job in an office, it was left to me to greet the PSE&G guy when he showed up and show him our boiler. I figured I could handle that.

Well, the doorbell rings Monday morning, and lo and behold, the gas company guy turns out to be a girl! Or rather, a woman. A large, African-American woman whom I will call Sheila.

I offer her a drink on this sweltering day, and she politely declines. So I show her downstairs to the boiler and prepare to head back upstairs to my computer. I figure she has her work to do, and I have mine.

"Not so fast!" she calls after me. "I need you to raise the thermostat so I can check the boiler while it's running."

"Sure, no problem," I reply.

"And then, come back downstairs with a pad and a pen and watch what I'm doing."

"I'm sorry, but is that absolutely necessary?" I ask in my innocence. "I've got work to do."

"Listen, lady, I hear this all the time from you housewives..."

I was about to explain to her about my working upstairs in this great study that we made out of the attic, and how I get important calls there, and I have a computer and a fax and a modem... but I thought better of it.

"All you ladies just think, 'hey, I don't need to know this stuff. My HUSBAND takes care of the boiler,'" she says, rather bitingly.

Yes, I'm thinking, that's exactly how I see the situation.

"Well, let's say your husband is away on a business trip, or he gets sick, or he just decides to walk out the door one morning and never come back? Then, what are you going to do? You're going to be alone in this house with your kids and the boiler will break down, and you won't know how to fix it. Is that what you want?"

Why no, it certainly is not. My husband having just spent more than a week in bed with pneumonia, the memory of his incapacitation was painfully fresh.

And so, I marched dutifully upstairs, turned up the thermostat to a toasty 80 degrees, got my pad and pen — no piece of scrap paper, a real legal pad — and returned, humbled, to my new teacher.

And there I sat, for 25 minutes, learning everything I never wanted to know about my boiler: about which valve to turn on to let in more water (never use the red one), about how many pounds of pressure it needs to maintain itself (12 to 15, never more than 30), about where the emergency switch is (to the left on the ceiling).

Allowing the water in is like making coffee, Sheila explained. "You know how, when you want to make four cups of coffee, you really have to put six cups of water in?" she asked helpfully, hoping to simplify things for me.

By the time Sheila left, I felt completely energized. I summarized the lecture over the phone to my husband, who was rendered speechless. When he came home that night, I gave him the full course, offering him a tip or two on how to maintain the boiler — which is, of course, what he will continue to do.

The boiler, and all the other mechanical whoozits that make our home function, are still his turf. I have no interest in encroaching on it.

But I have tasted from the tree of knowledge. And woe unto him who complains in the dead of winter that I am taxing the boiler by raising the thermostat too high.

The Gender Thing

July 1998

My not-quite two-year-old daughter's world is filled largely with cars, action figures, and sports paraphernalia. I didn't quite plan it that way, but these are the objects that have found their way into the hearts and haunts of her two older brothers. What's a girl supposed to do? She's gotta learn to play with the cards life has dealt her.

Recently, my mother bought a toy baby carriage as a gift. My daughter was playing with the carriage, mostly just wheeling it around the house. Then I noticed that she was looking for something. After a while, she picked up a rather large toy dump truck, examined it thoughtfully and then proceeded to cradle it in her arms, the way one would with a baby.

She gently brought the truck over to the carriage, placed it carefully inside and then covered it with a little blanket that came with the carriage. She pushed the carriage back and forth for a while, singing a warbly rendition of a lullaby.

Suddenly it hit me: my daughter needed a doll.

You'd think this might not be such a revelation. But for me, it was. I was never much of a doll person myself as a young girl, and with all the toys strewn around my house, I figured my daughter would make do with the material at hand. But even with the material available, she interacts differently. My boys always understood what to do with a truck; my daughter tried to nurture it.

Ever since I got married and started sharing my life and my apartment with a man, I gave up whatever notions I had about men and women being the same, after all. No doubt about it, the two genders are definitely from different planets. But was that any reason to feed into the conventional stereotypes about raising boys and girls?

I am, after all, an unabashed feminist. It's not just that I have encouraged my sons to help out in the kitchen and learn early on how to set the table. My husband and I have also tried, by our own example, to show our children that men and women are capable of performing all sorts of roles inside the house and outside in the world — in Jewish and secular settings.

My husband and I both work, we both cook, and we both change diapers. In the Jewish world, within the confines of our Modern Orthodox practice, we both try to participate in our community and in our observance at home. My husband says Kiddush on Friday night; I recite the blessing over the challah. We both set aside time to learn Torah; we both discuss the weekly Torah portion with the kids.

In fact, I had a satisfying chuckle recently when my husband was going over with my older son the concept of reading a particular Torah portion on your bar mitzvah. My son wanted to know what his bar mitzvah portion would be, what his brother's would be and then — without skipping a beat — what portion his sister would read for her bat mitzvah.

He also asked what my husband's portion was and what mine was. Well, I didn't have a bat mitzvah, I told my son. He was shocked, and immediately demanded to speak to Grandma and Grandpa to find out why I wasn't given a bat mitzvah. I didn't go into the history of the Modern Orthodox movement with him, but I was pleased at his reaction: sometimes, how we conduct ourselves and what we say may actually rub off on our children in the way we intended.

On the other hand, you never know. While I don't think I have consciously steered my children toward gender-specific toys or interests, the proof, as they say, is in the pudding. These days, my six-year-old son is reciting box scores to me over breakfast, my four-year-old son is obsessed with Spiderman, and my daughter is cradling a dump truck! So go figure.

It's true, I never bought dolls for my sons, but hey, I never bought one for my daughter, either. I did buy them stuffed animals, though, read them "Madeleine" books and take them to the "girl's shul" with me — their name for my women's *tefillah* group.

I do have a confession to make, however. My boys are no longer really interested in coming with me to the girl's shul. And while my daughter is still too young to know what any of this means, I take a special delight in bringing her with me instead. I secretly think it'll be more fun reading the Madeleine books to her, too. And you know what else? I finally bought her a doll.

Good Friday

January 1997

For Sabbath-observant Jews, the sixth day of the week presents a conundrum: no matter what time Shabbat begins — be it at 4 p.m. in the winter, or 8 p.m. in the summer — there is never enough time to prepare. And yet, no matter what time Shabbat begins, everyone is ready for it when it arrives.

This kind of affront to the laws of physics is one of the many little pleasures that I so enjoy about Fridays. For many Jews, Friday is a day of separation between our workaday lives and the sanctity of Shabbat. It is a day of transition, a day in which you immerse yourself in preparation for the sacred and yet still feel the sense of accomplishment from work and effort that can be rewarding in its own right.

I have a special relationship with Friday. It is a relationship I inherited from my mother. My mother held a variety of part-time jobs throughout most of my childhood. But she never worked on Friday.

Friday was her day to get ready for Shabbos. It was her day to do the shopping, the cooking, some cleaning. It was her day to speak to her sister, who lives in another state, and whom she doesn't see very often. "Good Friday," they would say to each other each week, in a takeoff on the Christian holy day.

As a child, what I liked best about my mother's Fridays were the pauses. In between chores, she would collapse for a few minutes in her favorite kitchen chair, sip some iced coffee, and just kind of be there for the asking. I would be home early from school and would look for excuses to join her during her pauses, just to enjoy the luxury of her sitting there and relaxing. In some ways it was a prelude to Shabbat, a day devoted entirely to rest, but these moments were somehow even more precious because they were stolen out of the flurry of activity that was Friday.

I have continued this Friday tradition. It started out quite inadvertently. My first job after graduate school involved working Sunday through Thursday. Every Friday brought with it the delightful sensation of playing hooky. It seemed as if I were the only person in New York City who had the day off. I would stroll down Broadway near where I lived, taking care of errands, luxuriating in front of shop windows, going in somewhere for a ridiculously late breakfast. By the time Shabbat rolled around and my roommate came rushing home from work like a madwoman, I was completely relaxed. She would glare.

This didn't last, of course. As I moved up through the ranks professionally, I was promoted to a more conventional work week. Friday then became a tense day, when I would spend whatever I had of the afternoon dreading the moment when I would have to leave hours before any of my colleagues. And of course, when I got home, I became that same madwoman dashing about before sunset, throwing things into the oven, checking the lights, jumping into the shower. I was a nervous wreck by the time Shabbat began.

And then came my first child. As my maternity leave drew to a close, I reached the conclusion that I couldn't, or perhaps just didn't, want to try to do it all. I wanted to get right on the "mommy track" and stay there until I was ready to get off. I was fortunate. I negotiated long and hard with my boss, and we finally agreed to a four-day work week. There was never any question in my mind as to which day I wanted off.

And so was born my own "Good Friday." No matter how crazy it is at work, I treat Friday like a holy day. I do not work. It is the day when I do my errands (especially since I live in

Bergen County, the only place north of the Mason-Dixon Line that still does not permit stores to be open on Sundays). It is the only day that I really cook — pasta and take-out will do during the week, but for Shabbos we always do it up. It is the day that I go for check-ups at the pediatrician. It is the day I volunteer to do things at my kids' schools. It is a very domestic day.

But it also *my* day. It is really the only day of the week when I get to dictate the terms. I've got my routines and my rhythm, and as long as they work, no one seems to mind what they are. While I'm cooking, I call one or two close friends from out of town and catch up. While I make my way around town, going to the supermarket, the butcher, the baker, the dry cleaner, I build my own little sense of community, chatting with the store owners, running into friends whom I might not otherwise see all week.

It is a day when I feel I have something to show for it when it's over. How many work days end with a feeling that you haven't accomplished what you set out to do? How many days with the kids are spent feeling like you've hit your head against a brick wall all day? On Fridays, come what may, Shabbat will arrive and I will have "made" it.

Of course, the day is a bit of a whirlwind, especially in these winter months. But there are the stolen moments, the cup of tea and the paper taken out while the two little ones are napping and the big one is still in school. The kids know that Friday afternoon is one long preparation. They know I'm home, but they also know I'm busy. Sometimes they help me make a favorite recipe, sometimes they help set the table, sometimes they just play or watch TV.

But there are also the pauses — like when each of them comes home from school laden with all his art projects of the week and we go over each one together; or when one of them sidles up to me as I take a break in my kitchen chair, and just tells me what's what.

And, during one of the pauses every Friday, I call my mother. And we always wish each other a very Good Friday.

A Round-Trip Ticket to School

November 1996

A couple of months ago, I committed one of the most unspeakable acts of parenthood: I rose up early one morning, took my first-born child — my *bechor* — and offered him up to that moving den of iniquity, the school bus.

There he was, lunch box in hand, knapsack on his back, address and phone number pinned in four different places on his chest. Five years old, and he was positively beaming with pride as he ascended those bus steps for the first time.

And there I was, standing at the curb, blubbering like an idiot, waving to him through my tears and using every ounce of my strength to restrain myself from leaping on board and warning every kid not to lay a hand, or a nasty word, on my son. Then I would sit down beside him, and just this once, go with him to school.

And then the bus drove out of sight, and he was gone. I work, so I can't say this is the first time that he and I have spent our days apart. But he is in "big school" now, a Jewish day school where the days are long and crowded with a dual curriculum. This is the first time that my son is spending practically his entire day in his own life, guided by its own rules and peopled by his own friends and teachers. Except in rough outline, I really have no idea what he does all day.

Very quickly, I learned that this new world of his is impervious to outsiders like myself. Direct, open-ended questions such as, "What did you do in school today?" are generally greeted with one of the following helpful responses: a) I don't remember; b) I don't want to tell you; or, that most insidious, pre-adolescent response, c) Nothing.

"Permission to treat as a hostile witness, Your Honor?" (This always seems to work on "Law and Order.")

I know these are time-honored answers, probably written down in a secret "How to Grow Up and Drive Your Parents Crazy" book circulated among children of each generation and then promptly forgotten by those children when they reach adulthood. As parents, these same former children all seem to read the companion book, "How to Ask Your Kids Dumb, Unanswerable Questions."

So I am learning. I try to ask targeted, indirect, non-threatening questions, like: "Did you have recess in the playground or in the gym today?" This approach, of course, can only take me so far.

Instead, I am learning mostly to wait; to wait and to listen. I listen for the sounds of his school day; they emerge in the most delightful, unexpected ways. Like the other night, as we were reading a library book, he turns to me and informs me that in his school library, you take books out differently than in the library that we go to together. He then gives me an unsolicited, detailed account of his class's visit to the school library.

Because he is in a Jewish day school, the sights and sounds of his school day have begun to infiltrate every aspect of our observance. He knows the blessing over every food; he recites the *"Shema"* before going to sleep; and in keeping with the weekly Torah portion, which is now in the Book of Genesis, he is matter-of-factly letting me in on the story of Creation as it unfolds for him.

But for me, it is the singing that truly reassures me. Each time he comes home with a new song, I somehow feel that I have a sense of where he's been all day. And I know that where he's been is very similar to where I was oh, about 30 years ago. The songs come ricocheting back across time to me: I send him off in the morning on the school bus, and he comes back in the afternoon with the songs that filled my own youth and that of young Jews through the generations.

Granted, the exact words and melodies have changed somewhat, but the themes are enduring. My son sings about God creating the world; about not working on Shabbat; about "*Dovid Melech Yisrael*." (Raise your hand if the line, "Chai, chai, pizza pie," means anything to you; my son thought it was hysterical.)

He doesn't perform the songs; usually I catch him singing while he is playing with his cars or procrastinating over dinner. The tunes are seeping into his life, the way they had in mine. He is absolutely amazed when I am able to join in with him and sing along. I am impressed that after all these years I still remember the words.

But these are the songs that last. Some are cute and help bring vast ideas into focus for a child; others are profound and the children do not yet even understand the words. But the tunes and the associations, I see, will last a lifetime. And they will bind us, in some instinctive way, to everyone else who can sing along.

The other night in the bathtub, I heard my son singing the "*Hatikvah*" at the top of his lungs. I could not believe my ears. I ran into the bathroom and asked him what song he was singing. "The Israel song," he said simply, somewhat surprised that I didn't seem to know this one.

"*Od lo avdah tikvataynu*," he warbled, blissfully ignorant of the history behind these words; "Our hope is not yet lost." With five-year-olds belting this out in the bathtub, our hope is indeed very much alive.

His Brother's Keeper

March 1999

"Okay, what's the 'chedule tomowwow?"

My two boys have settled in for the night, the younger on the bottom bunk, the older one on top. I have helped them brush their teeth, read them a story, and kissed them goodnight. I then beat a hasty retreat from their room; "my" part of the evening has begun and there are phone calls to return and bills to pay.

But, as I discovered one night recently, my boys have their own post-parent evening rituals, as well. I needed to do some things in my study, which is near their room. They must have waited a few minutes till they heard my footsteps recede, and then my younger son proceeded to pose the above question to his older brother.

"Well, tomorrow we're going to school. We'll probably learn about Purim. Then, after school, Mama is coming home early and we're going to the dentist."

"What do you do at the dentist?"

"Well, he's going to count your teeth. And he's going to make sure you're brushing well. We better brush our teeth really well in the morning." "Do you like Sammy Sosa or Mark McGuire?"

And so on. They chatted like that for what must have been at least a half-hour, quietly, contentedly. Since that night, I've been listening, and I realize something like this conversation takes place almost every evening.

Sometimes, their little sister will wander in, lonely in her own room, and just sit on the floor listening. Sometimes my oldest, a new reader, will show off his skills and read aloud to his siblings.

After 8 p.m., it seems, we are leading parallel lives. My husband and I will be downstairs eating a late dinner and filling each other in on our day, while my children are upstairs in their room, discussing how their own days are filled.

Of course, my children play with each other during the day. That's one of the reasons I wanted them each to have siblings. And I encourage this, naturally. But this night-time ritual is entirely of their own making, and does not involve me or my husband at all.

In fact, I think it thrives because we are not there. And I need to get used to the idea that my children are creating a relationship with each other, one that will almost surely outlast the ones that they have with their parents.

Relationships among siblings are never simple, as anyone with a brother or sister will attest. They are among the most complex and tangled ones we have, but they are also probably the longest lasting and most deeply rooted.

There's only so much parents can do to shape this relationship, especially as our children grow. At this young stage in my children's relationship to one another, my approach has been to encourage a closeness, and also to stand back.

My two boys are only two years apart, their sister only three years younger. They often fight, they vie for mine and my husband's attention, and even at their tender ages (seven, five, and two), they covet their own space. But through it all, they are developing a bond that is resilient.

On Shabbat afternoon, the two boys in particular can play for hours with each other, setting up rules for their action figures and schedules for their car races. When we travel to a new place, they almost instinctively hold each other's hands as we enter a hotel or an unfamiliar home. When my younger son started pre-K this year, it was his big brother who showed him around the school and gave him the lowdown on his teachers.

I am not naive enough to think the road ahead will be as smooth. I already know how different their personalities are; they will clash at points and perhaps grow distant at other points. I can only hope that they will share in each other joys and stand beside each other during the hard times. There will be times when they will each serve as each other's best comfort.

We are entering now a season of family; the Passover seder reunites families like almost no other holiday ritual can. Many of us make a point of getting together with our adult siblings and their families; my husband jokes that when my brother and I sing our old seder melodies together, it is as if we are adolescents again, competing to see who can sing loudest or fastest. But for us, at least, these are melodies that bind us to our parents' home, to our youth, and to each other.

My children now are writing their own tunes; I can only hope they keep singing them for many years to come.

For Auld Lang Syne

June 1999

I had the luxury recently to spend a few days surrounded by old friends. Some friends from my post-college, early adulthood years came to town for the holiday weekend. By coincidence, a former high school classmate decided to organize a mini-reunion that Sunday in honor of the 20th anniversary of our graduation from high school.

Among other epiphanies that came to me that weekend, it hit me that I have reached the age where friendships that began after high school can already be nearly 20 years old. And yes, age, and the passage of time, was a big theme that ran through those few days.

But mostly, our conversations were grounded very much in the present. Our lives, to a large extent, have so far taken remarkably similar courses. We are all married, with children. We are all working in the professions for which we trained, but mostly on a "Mommy-track" kind of schedule. We are all religiously observant, having not veered very far in either direction from the Modern Orthodox lifestyle in which we were raised. And we are all still pretty close to our parents.

In short, we are not a terribly remarkable group. We fit comfortably into our respective communities. And yet we know each other in ways that belie this superficial sameness. We know all the quirks and all the wrinkles. We know the dark recesses of each other's pasts — the guys we were madly in love with before we met our husbands; the restaurants we ate in before we became truly kosher; the dreams we aspired to before we took our jobs.

And oh, do we love to talk. I'm not sure what most men do when they get together — my husband and his friends tend to rent dumb movies — but my female friends and I just simply like to talk.

As a result, as one friend's husband used to joke when he was first introduced to his wife's friends, "there are no secrets" among us. This is sometimes a frightening thought, and sometimes a deeply comforting one. While we have all, more or less, made peace with our current lives, we each have hopes and aspirations and dreams and conflicts and struggles and hurts that are difficult to share with people who know us only in our present incarnations.

Among ourselves, we can speak in shorthand — to an outsider, it may sound like we are speaking in tongues; we can make references to events and people without explanation; we can laugh at punchlines without bothering with the jokes. And, to our chagrin sometimes, we cannot embellish or reinvent the past with one another. We must speak the truth, and while that can be alarming in polite society, it can also be refreshing.

I can ask an old friend, whom I see only rarely, do you still think of building your own practice — a question that may never have occurred to her next-door neighbor whom she sees every day — because I know what went into her years of training. And another friend could ask me, whatever happened to making aliyah, because she knows how important that used to be to me.

We can sit around and gossip about former classmates whose lives are more scandalous than our own. But we also all fall silent when we learn that another friend's mother is very ill — and not just because she is a friend, but because we also really know her mother.

And since our lives are very similar, we can also gain strength and support, and some helpful hints, on how to cope with the conflicting demands of jobs and motherhood and wifehood and daughterhood that so dominate our daily existence. It is good to step back and realize we are not alone in these struggles.

Whatever it was that forged these friendships 20 years ago or more — and each one has its own tale — these are the ones that have withstood the test of time. The older I get, the more precious they have become to me. I think of each one as a well, from which I can periodically, if not as often as I would like, draw my sustenance.

In each friendship lies a part of me, a part that may have been revealed in a long, winding 2 a.m. dorm-room conversation, or in a brief, emotionally charged moment during the illness of a parent. To re-connect with an old friend is like re-connecting with a part of myself, with a part of who I was at a particular time and who I had wanted to be.

But the friendships that really last are the ones that are not limited to nostalgia. The ones that last continue to draw on this depth, on this shared history, but they are also able to grow and to adapt. And as they grow, they are broadened and lengthened and strengthened. In the daily rush of existence, they stand — often in the background — like a rock, as solid as gold.

Kids of the Book

August 1999

I've been having the most delightful series of arguments with my seven-year-old son in recent weeks.

"Shut the light off. It's after 9 o'clock and it's time to get to sleep!"

"Oh, please, Mama! Just one more chapter!"

"Okay, one more, and that's it."

Fifteen minutes elapse. "I still see the light on. What's going on?"

"Just a few more pages and I'm finished with the book. Please?!"

And so on. On many nights, after this exchange, he will suddenly appear downstairs, flush with excitement. "I finished the book. It was a mystery! I've got to tell you what happened!"

While I do not relish the sight of my pajama-clad son, who has to be woken up for camp the next morning at 7:30, appearing before me at 10 p.m., I cannot deny that I take a deep pride and pleasure in his reasons for being there.

He just finished first grade this year, and somewhere in the last few months, reading has taken hold. He grabs the sports section every morning as my husband brings the paper in. He reads the backs of cereal boxes out loud over breakfast. He reads street signs, license plates, and billboards as we walk or drive outside.

But mostly, he is reading books. And he is reading because he wants to, because he is enjoying himself, and yes, because he feels a sense of accomplishment. He is excited by the worlds opened up by the book about outer space, he anticipates the mysteries being solved in his adventure series, and he gets a kick out of the fact that the TV character "Arthur" actually has a bunch of books to his credit, too. And this, I know, is only the beginning.

Okay, so what mother does not take pride in her child reading? And what Jewish mother, in particular? It was, after all, my mother — hands down, the most well-read person I know — who introduced me to a love of reading, feeding and cultivating my passion with weekly visits to the library and much less stringent rules about how late you could stay up if you were in the middle of a good book.

But by "Jewish mother," I don't mean to just play to the stereotype of our tribe being more bookish or scholarly. We are the People of the Book, and this expression, despite its more generalized usage, does refer to a particular Book. My son this year has also learned to read Hebrew. When he recites the Kiddush over wine on Friday nights or opens his brand-new siddur to pray in the morning, the sight of his reading Hebrew and the sound of his words echo through the generations.

As the author and critic Leon Wieseltier has pointed out, we live in an age of unprecedented Jewish illiteracy. Unfortunately, my son, at age seven, knows more Hebrew than most adult American Jews today. His knowledge of Hebrew is a priority for me and my husband. We know that as many doors as his English literacy will open for him, his understanding of Hebrew will one day take him on journeys not only in prayer, but also through the Torah, the Talmud, and the rabbinical canon. It will make him feel at home in Israel and make Israel always be a part of his home. It will take him forward in his own growth, and back, through the reaches of Jewish history.

And in my family, there is yet another dimension still to this literacy thing. I am a writer and a journalist; I have spent my entire adult life grappling with the written word. But I am not the first in my family to have done so. My father too is a writer.

True, he earned his living in the garment district; but that was a fluke of fate. He had written for Yiddish newspapers in Poland before the war, and it took him 40 years to retire from his day job and pick up where he left off. He now writes regularly for a Yiddish newspaper in New York.

With this heritage, perhaps it should not have come as such a surprise to me when my son announced recently that he was starting his own newspaper. In school, he and his classmates kept a daily journal. But when school let out for the summer, he realized that he would have no regular outlet in which to record his activities and thoughts. And so he decided he would produce a daily "family newspaper," recording the annals of our family over the summer.

It appears almost every morning (our subscription lapses from time to time) on the kitchen table, along with *The New York Times*. As an old newspaperwoman myself, I'm not sure if I should be *schepping nachas* or worrying about his future.

This newspaper is his, of course, as are the books he is reading. But I look forward to sharing with him, and my other children, the most engaging books of my own childhood as well as the passion and satisfaction of writing a story well told. I can imagine no greater satisfaction as a parent than watching as my children's imaginations take flight and their dreams begin to soar.

When I'm a Mom

June 2000

"I want to be a mom when I grow up," my not-quite-four-year-old daughter told me recently, while I was cleaning up in the kitchen and she was playing nearby.

"That's nice," I replied somewhat absentmindedly, though pleased that she thought motherhood a worthwhile aspiration.

Then she went for the jugular. "But when I'm a mom, I'm not going to go to work. I'm going to stay home with the children."

And so, after blithely stabbing me through the heart, my daughter returned to her dollhouse.

This exchange took place during a sabbatical week that I was taking between jobs. I was about to start a new job that promised me better hours and a saner life than I had previously. I was feeling very self-righteous that week: I had made a decision in my professional life that was intended to improve the quality of my family's life. My family was supposed to appreciate me for that. And yet here was my daughter basically repudiating the whole effort. Forget the delicate balancing act, she seemed to be saying. Just stay home already!

I'm not sure if too much has been written or not enough could ever be written on the overwrought subject of working mothers (you don't hear much about "working fathers," do you?). I've been at this for nearly nine years now, and not a day goes by without my encountering at least one incident, comment, or thought that challenges me to the core.

The challenges range from the logistical — if I go to my son's school for a special program in the morning, and thus get into work late, how do I make it home in time to do karate carpool?; to the philosophical — if I believe that homework should be done upon arrival home from school, shouldn't I be home at that hour?; to the sublime — how can I ever advance my career and still be home for dinner?

And they work both ways. Yes, it is more wrenching for me to think of all the childhood milestones I have missed, but I must admit that it is not always easy to let the potential promotions and career-enhancing moves pass me by.

As soon as my first child was born, I jumped on the Mommy track and have never gotten off. What that means varies based on the day of the week. On those days when I am productive in the office, and still get home in time for dinner, homework, and baths — I feel I have the best of both worlds. I don't work full time but I do have a career and an ample amount of time to spend with my kids. And then there are the days when I run out the door of my office, knowing that I am going to miss an important phone call, only to miss my bus, and get home in time to be greeted by an angry eight-year-old who is late for his basketball practice. Then I feel I've got two short ends of a stick.

The guilt is pervasive — I'm not doing enough for my family and I'm not pulling my weight at work. And my parents, friends, community? Where do they fit in? I also know that I am living in a house of cards. Pull my babysitter out from under me, and the whole thing falls apart. Throw in bad weather and stalled traffic and I fall apart.

So why do I persist in this dual role? One reason is money. That's a simple and honest response, but not a complete one. Like many women, I have made my choices, and I am fortunate because they have been mine to make. I want to work. That's the truth. And I am doubly fortunate because I love what I do.

There is no substitute for the time we spend with our children. And I don't just mean "quality time"; I mean the old-fashioned kind of time, "quantity time," where more really is better. But to put aside all our other interests and priorities would leave many of us wanting.

We all draw our lines at different points in the sand. Some mothers — and fathers, too — find it anathema to miss anything in their children's daily lives, from birth through adolescence. Others draw the line at the hour that the school bus comes home, or the dinner hour, or the bedtime hour. I am in no position to judge others. But it is my responsibility to judge myself and know where to draw my own lines.

And that is perhaps the key to this whole juggling act: to be comfortable with the choices we make, to try to ensure that they work for ourselves and our families, and to understand and accept what it is that we gain and what we give up every time we choose one option over another.

Maybe by the time my daughter grows up, somebody will have figured out the perfect solution to this heart-wrenching puzzle. But I doubt it. I suspect women will always have to make these difficult choices, in one form or another. I hope I have the courage of my convictions when my daughter makes hers — even if she chooses to stay home with the children.

Four-stalling the Future

August 2000

My "baby" turned four last week, and the number sticks in my throat.

There's a story behind this number.

Many moons ago, when I was a new mother, my husband and I decided go to Florida for a few days with our then four-month-old son. We'd been there before, but, of course, we did not realize how different the trip would be with an infant. Suffice it to say that by Friday night, when I was asked to wait in the hotel lobby with the baby rather than enter the makeshift shul, I was feeling overwhelmed and resentful.

So I sat down next to a slightly older woman, who had her hair covered with a wig, and I kept a close eye on my precious darling. Of course, being four months old, he couldn't exactly go anywhere, so my attention began to turn to this woman. Every two minutes, it seemed, another child was running over to her. All ages, all genders. "Mommy, can I have a pretzel?" "Mommy, she hit me!" "Mommy, we're going to play outside," etc.

I watched, awestruck, as she took this all in stride, never raising her voice, never getting frazzled. In fact, while I had gotten up half-a-dozen times during this flurry of activity to adjust my son's blanket or dangle a toy in front of him, she had not actually lifted a finger. This woman and I had not exchanged a word, but guessing, I suppose, what I was thinking, she turned to me at a quiet moment, and said with authority: "It really doesn't matter how many you have, as long as they're over four."

And I never even knew her name.

Well, ever since then, the number four has loomed as the demarcation point.

Until you're four, you're a baby, or a toddler, or a preschooler. But, as my husband is fond of saying, you are not really a person. The human race is distinguished from the rest of the animal kingdom by its ability to use reason; when you hit four, you begin to see the dawning of that powerful tool.

The child can be reasoned with, cajoled, bribed — whatever it takes. He or she is ready to enter the human race. They're also ready to be sent off to school for a good chunk of the day. If that's not the mark of being civilized, what is?

From that day in Florida forward, I could not wait for my son to turn four. I marked the days until he would become a bona fide kid. Not only would he be independent and reasonable at that point, but he would no longer need such accoutrements that bog you down every time you leave the house — the stroller, the diaper bag, the special toy or stuffed animal you can never afford to be without.

And sure enough, as both he and then his younger brother reached that milestone, I did indeed see the benefits. They were able to entertain themselves, they acquired a circle of friends, they went to the bathroom without assistance, they asked fun questions and engaged in more interesting conversations. At each of their four-year-old birthday parties, I felt I had gotten over the proverbial hump.

But not so with my youngest. With her, I wanted time to stand still. I did not want her to move into kid-dom. I wanted to hold on to her babyhood, or toddlerhood, and all that those stages imply. The flip side of attaining the age of reason is that you're just not as cute anymore. And you don't let your mother hug you in public quite so often.

I kicked my two big ones out of their strollers as soon as they could walk; she's still riding around like a princess. I weaned the other two from their special objects as soon as they went off to preschool; she is still allowed her blankie. This one even had to toilet-train herself; I just wasn't ready when she started showing interest. So sue me.

As I think any parent can attest, the youngest is just different. You savor every stage just that much more, knowing it might be your last opportunity to do so. (Note to family and friends: I know, never say never.)

I find myself cuddling with her more, babying her more, holding her more tightly. I have more of a chance to do this, since my older two are indeed more independent and out of the house more or busy with their own interests and friends. There are many a Shabbat morning now when she and I are the only ones in the house. I should be encouraging her to go to shul with her father, the way I was so anxious to do with her big brothers. But I don't. I let her linger with me, getting things ready for lunch or browsing through the Sunday *Times*.

Of course, I know what I am trying to hold onto. I am trying to hold onto her youth, and my own. The fact that I am rapidly approaching 40 myself probably doesn't help. A chapter is closing, and while it's been a very time-consuming, all-encompassing, physically and emotionally draining chapter — it's also been the most rewarding one of my life. These years have passed oh so quickly. As another wise, anonymous woman once said to me years ago, as she passed me struggling to get in the door of the library with my two younger ones in a double stroller and my oldest walking nearby: "The days are long — but the time is short."

To Sleepaway Camp and Beyond

July 2002

The signs are all there. A grown woman counting and re-counting underwear and socks. Name tags appearing out of nowhere, in search of t-shirts, shorts, and other sundry items that need to have them ironed on. Old sheets, which have not seen the light of day in years, being pulled out of the linen closet and re-marketed as "good as new."

In a few short weeks, I will commit one of the more unspeakable acts of parenthood: I will rise up early one morning, take my first-born child, my *bechor*, and offer him up to that den of iniquity in the mountains: sleepaway camp. And yes, if you haven't already guessed it, this is his and my first time.

Oh, I went to sleepaway camp myself, for no fewer than nine summers. But that was different. I wasn't the parent. It's one thing for the kid to be excited, to look forward to being on his own, in a new environment, making new friends, etc., etc. But why do we parents voluntarily send away our young for a month or two at a time?

I suppose the benefits are not that hard to figure out. First and foremost: your kid is away for a month or two. What's not to like? You don't have to deal with your adolescent or pre-adolescent, and he doesn't have to deal with you. The absence of one, I am told, also changes the dynamics of the kids left behind, easing the tension of sibling rivalry, allowing the other kids to shine and allowing you to pay more attention to them. Clearly, once you have two or more gone for the summer, even, perchance the whole lot of them — you have a bona fide vacation on your hands. For the mere price of half a year's tuition at a Jewish day school, you can sit in your backyard all summer and marvel at how peaceful it is without the kids. Then, of course, you might start wondering why you even have a backyard, but that's another story. (You apartment dwellers, I guess, wander through the empty rooms — same basic idea.)

But if it's a vacation we're after, it seems to me we're sending away the wrong kids. It's the younger kids that require the most work; why not send them away? They're the ones that still need help getting dressed in the morning and still have tantrums when their Barbie dolls get messed up. What's the use in sending away the only one who can take a shower by himself? Not to mention the only one who can babysit the others?

Okay, okay, I know. We send our kids to camp for much the same reasons that we will one day send them off to college and beyond. They need to be on their own, they need to grow in ways that parents are often not best suited for, they need to be let go of.

But it is also true that this really is a time in their lives when we grow to enjoy their company more and more. My nearly 12-year-old, the one I am banishing for a month this summer, has turned into a real delight. Of course, I have always delighted in my children. But at each stage, you relate to them in a different way. My son is now reaching the age where I can enjoy him as a companion. Besides being able to fix anything wrong with my computer, he has become an engaging conversationalist and an avid reader eager to discuss what he is absorbing every day. True, the Yankees' box scores are not always my favorite topic of discussion. But, in response to my seeming indifference to the sports headlines of the day, he is learning to appreciate my dry sense of humor, and developing a rather wry one of his own.

It is such a pleasure watching him come into his own, in ways I had always hoped for him, and in other, more surprising ways that are even more enchanting. And it is at this juncture that I am supposed to part with him for a month? Yes, I realize, it is exactly at this juncture. Though I am being deprived the enjoyment of his company for a time, I know that he is ready to engage the world, on his own terms. Granted, a Jewish sleep-away camp is not exactly the wide, wide world, nor is camp the right place for every kid.

But going away for a month is definitely a step toward independence. And it is a step that my son very much wants to take. With mine and my husband's support and encouragement, I hope it is a step away from us that will eventually lead him back to us, with ties that much richer for the experience.

The Next Forty

June 2001

So I'm turning 40 this month. I know all you cynics will say, 'It's just a number. Get over it.' But I am at heart a romantic, and I've chosen instead to wallow in it.

In fact, I've been preparing to be depressed for almost a year now. As a friend of mine remarked recently, when you tell people you're 39, they kind of look at you knowingly, like, who do you think you are, Jack Benny? So you basically get a year to stave off the reality of the number while practicing being 40 in the eyes of the world.

And what does 40 connote? Forty means bifocals. Forty means gray hair, wrinkles, mammograms. Forty means a different marketing demographic. I got all excited recently when an athletic shoe company offered free sneakers to women at my firm who would participate in a focus group — until I realized they only wanted women between the ages of 24 to 39.

No matter how you slice it, 40 is middle-aged. Interestingly, my mother, may she live to 120, is the one who most objects to this characterization, since she, of course, cannot be the mother of a middle-aged woman. But middle-aged I am, and besides all the physical manifestations that mark this milestone, there are the emotional ones, as well. If I have, in a best-case scenario, reached the middle of my life, then that means that half my life is over. Now if that's not enough to give one pause, I don't know what is.

And that's what I'm doing as 40 approaches. I am pausing. There are choices you make in your first 40 years — and some that are made for you — that inevitably shape the next 40. So I am coming to grips with the dreams that will never be. I never did take that year off after school to travel the world, relying only on my wits and a backpack. I never tried my hand at writing a novel before the need to earn a real paycheck came along. I didn't make aliyah before putting down roots in America. Fame and fortune may have forever eluded me.

But the good thing about turning 40 is that, in a way, your world narrows and draws inward. And you realize that your dreams and aspirations have changed along the way. Where once I longed to strike out on my own, live somewhere where no one knew me, and have the chance to reinvent myself, I now savor being part of a community where some people have known me for 20 years and more. Where once I thrived on working 12-hour days and chasing hot stories and the glory that came with them, I now long only to be home for dinner and to write articles that are more reflective. Where once I wanted to change the whole world, I now focus more on the world in which I can realistically effect change — myself, my family, my community.

Is this all some lame rationalization for my own less-than-glamorous existence? Or is it a sign of maturity and a sense of being comfortable with who I am? Probably a combination of both. I recently had the great pleasure of spending the weekend with some old, dear friends whom I see rarely, but cherish deeply. In the wee hours of many nights 20 years ago, we confided to each other our loftiest ambitions and innermost fears, as all the world lay before us. And now, 20 years later, we have suffered losses, taken on great responsibilities, and closed some doors forever, but, still laughing and crying late into the night, we have remained essentially the same individuals. I took great comfort in that.

Truth be told, I am a lot happier now than when I was 20. Thanks to my husband, I have not felt alone in more than 12 years. And thanks to my children, I have experienced a kind of love I never even knew existed. Yes, I have reached that point in life when not all roads are open to me, when some opportunities have been forever missed. A lot of questions that obsessed me when I was younger have been answered — I know who I married, I know who my children are, I know where I live, and I know what career I'm in.

But there are still many questions to ask, and many answers yet to discover. As I kick off the next 40 years, my old wanderlust has returned. Some people go off to some exotic locale for their 40th — Bali, or the south of France, or Hawaii. Me, I'm going to Poland. Back to where it all started.

This is my first time traveling without the husband and kids and I will guiltily admit that I am looking forward to that feeling from my youth, when I could travel freely and feel responsible to no one but myself. But I also know that I could not have taken this trip when I was younger. I needed to be where I am today. I needed to feel that I am not wandering alone, that I am a part of something real and beloved, that I have built something for myself in this world, and that there is much for which to come home.

It Takes a Village

February 2002

"You've got cancer." The words still reverberate, sending shockwaves of despair. They are words none of us is ever prepared to hear. I certainly wasn't, when they were told to me by my doctor after what I thought was a routine test two months ago.

With these words, my life as I knew it ended, and I entered the alternate universe inhabited by the very ill. It is not a pretty world and I would not invite any of you to join me in it. Believe me, I will spare you the details.

But as much as you, dear readers, have allowed me to share the vagaries of my life with you over the years, I will ask you to indulge me yet again. I have wrestled long and hard over whether to write about my illness.

Finally, I realized, I can think of no other response to it. Writing is what I do. Not to write now is tantamount to letting cancer defeat yet another part of me.

So join me, if you will, on this new voyage; it is not one I would have ever wished for, but it is no less full of wonder than anything I ever encountered in my "normal" life. I have learned, for example, that, in the immortal words of Hillary Clinton: It takes a village. In my case, it is the village of Teaneck, N.J., along with various other members of my virtual village in far-flung places such as Manhattan and Israel. I left my beloved New York City for this New Jersey village eight years ago, kicking and screaming all the way about the horrors of living in a close-knit, homogeneous suburb where everybody knows your business.

Well, all I can say is, thank God for this close-knit, homogeneous suburb where everyone knows your business. On any number of occasions in the past two months, the wonderful individuals who make up this community have literally saved my life, or at least enhanced my family's existence while I needed to tend to life-saving measures. Some are old, dear friends whose goodness I have relied on for many years; some are people I barely know, motivated, I must assume, by the kindness of their hearts.

Consider this, then, an open thank you card to all those who have stepped forward in the past few weeks. You stand as an inspiration. Humbled, I realize how little I knew about true *chesed* — an act of kindness that cannot be returned in kind. It can make all the difference in the world.

For every phone call filled with good wishes; for every card that arrived in the mail; for every visit in the hospital; for every kugel lovingly brought over on a Friday afternoon; for every carpool picked up and dropped off without a word of complaint; for every offer of a play-date for one of my kids; for every emergency "sleepover" that had to be arranged on a moment's notice; for every book dropped off as a source of inspiration or merely distraction; for every prayer or Psalm said on my behalf; for every extra trip to the supermarket or bakery carried out with the lame excuse, "Oh, I'm going there anyway" — for all these and more, I thank you from the bottom of my heart.

There's my doctor-neighbor down the block who checks up on me every day and has turned into my guardian angel; the other neighbor, also a doctor, who personally wheeled me to my hospital room when she discovered I had been left waiting in the X-ray area; the friend, who, learning that I was once again in the emergency room in New York, but had to make it to Washington for an appointment with a specialist the next morning, spent all night driving me down because my husband was too exhausted. And then there are the friends in Washington who provided me and my family with a home away from home.

There's the friend who has twice accompanied me and my husband to the emergency room, and his wife, who then goes immediately to check on my kids; there are the friends who have taken on coordinating all these other efforts; and there are the virtual strangers who have lent us their expertise simply because they live in the community and know something about my disease.

Words cannot capture the gratitude that I feel. Suffice it to say that in the midst of all my pain and heartache, these gestures, large and small, have made me feel also truly blessed. I have always considered myself fairly self-reliant and, at first, neither my husband nor I felt comfortable accepting all these kindnesses. I felt like nothing more than the town charity project.

But I am learning, in part because I have no choice. I am learning to appreciate that people do good things in all kinds of situations for all kinds of reasons. And it is not for me to question how or why. As one friend said to me, all this good being generated can only lead to more good.

V'khayn yehi ratzon — And let it be so.

In My Life

June 2002

It's the Beatles, stupid.

That's what I felt like one day recently when my fourth-grader came home from school humming a somewhat mangled but vaguely familiar tune. He and his classmates had been assigned to read a biography of someone they admired and present the person's life story in a creative fashion to the rest of the class. My son picked Albert Einstein, but that's another story. Another kid — whose parents had obviously brought him up well — had picked the Beatles and played for the class a CD with some of the group's best-known songs.

So there's my son humming "Ob-La-Di, Ob-la-da," and it suddenly hits me what a negligent parent I've been. Why hadn't I ever introduced my children to the finer things in life, not to mention one of the seminal influences of my youth?

There is no time like the present, I decided. Like a woman possessed, I threw all caution and homework to the wind, and dragged my son down to the basement with me. "We're going to dig out some of my old albums," I told him excitedly. "OK, Mama," he said, gamely trying to play along. "But what's an album?" Other 40-year-olds might have given up at this point. But I was determined to relive my youth with my first-born.

Yes, we still have a turntable. As I dusted off a few albums and put one favorite on, I explained to my son and his two siblings who the Beatles were, how my best friend and her older brother first introduced me to them back when I was about my son's age, and how important they were to my generation and beyond. I don't think my kids had ever seen me this way before. At first, they just stared as I sang along with the songs, almost oblivious to them and to my middle-aged suburban surroundings; then they started laughing and smiling as I yanked them up off the couch and began dancing around the room with them. When my bewildered husband came home from work a short time later, I pulled him onto my makeshift dance floor and twirled him around to the tune of "Eight Days a Week."

My kids were delighted and transfixed; my husband and I were transported back to a time when we didn't even know each other. But we knew other things in those days, or at least we thought we did. I knew my place in the universe that encompassed school, camp, and family. I knew that my parents were the bedrock of my existence; I knew who my best friend was, who my "clique" was in school, and what I wanted to be when I grew up. Of course, all those things would change over time, and the Beatles and the culture they helped spawn were no small part of the changes that would put my world, and the whole world, into flux.

But there was a time and a place when I could count on certain certainties and they helped shape who I am to this day. Perhaps the only silver lining to having been diagnosed with cancer several months ago is that I have reconnected in unexpected ways with people from all walks of my life, but most particularly, with old, dear, and long out-of-touch friends.

If I may quote from a recent letter from that same best friend who introduced me to the Beatles so long ago — and with whom I have not been in touch in years: "For me, talking to old friends has this kind of magical power to make me real — not just me, sitting here at this moment, but the me that's been me all along, since the very beginning of me.... Whatever else we may be today, the two little girls we were then are here with us now. They never left us." (She was an aspiring writer, too.)

I know this to be true because each time I receive a letter like hers or a phone call from someone I learned with in Israel or an e-mail from a college friend, the connection is instant. The conversations are seamless and without pause. Yes, there's the catching up to do in terms of facts and figures: How many kids do you have? What kind of work are you doing? But the meat of the conversation comes straight from the heart. It's almost a conversation that's being picked up where it was left off. Whatever it was that attracted us to each other is still there. The circumstances of our current lives, however different they may now be, seem almost irrelevant.

These connections and the memories they stir up remind us of who we are, at the core. They may make me long for the time in my life when the future stretched before me so bright and so limitless. But they also help deepen my present and make me realize that I am a sum of all my experiences, not just the more recent ones. And I am so much richer for all the connections I've made over the years. So, to go back to the Fab Four:

"There are places I remember all my life,
Though some have changed. Some forever, not for better,
Some have gone and some remain.
All these places had their moments
With lovers and friends I still can recall.
Some are dead and some are living.
In my life I've loved them all."

Musings on Holidays and Faith

Oh My God!

August 1996

Well, my son finally asked the question. You know, THE question. The one where you look at your spouse and say, "You answer this one — he's your son" and your spouse looks at you and says, "Oh, no. I'm not touching this one. He's *your* son."

The question, of course, is the God question. Compared to this one, I think the birds and the bees will be a cakewalk.

"What is God?" my son asked one day out of the blue. At least he did not commit the sin of anthropomorphism, as some of my friends' children have, asking their parents, "Who is God?"

In fact, a very unscientific poll among some of my friends revealed that keying the answer to the exact question is part of the dilemma itself.

One friend's daughter was taught in school the ubiquitous song, "Hashem is here, Hashem is there, Hashem is really everywhere" — which goes a long way toward explaining where God is. But it doesn't do much by way of what or who.

Another friend told her daughter that "Hashem lives in our hearts" — a more poetic take on the "where" formulation — but was then stumped when her daughter asked, "What happens when our hearts stop?"

Someone else I know tells her children that God makes all the good things in this world. Even putting aside the existential quandaries presented by this response, it tells us what God does for a living, but again, does not really deal with the essential who or what of God.

And then there is the troublesome "why" formulation. When my son was taught in school that God made the whole world and everything in it, he spent the next several weeks asking why God made oil tankers with 18 wheels; why God made the toilet overflow right before Shabbat (a question that passed through my own head at the time); and why God made Daddy have to stay late at work so often.

When I told my younger son that the flowers outside our house were yellow and he, kind of randomly, asked "why?", his newly theologically informed big brother volunteered, "because God made them that way." I guess I couldn't have said it better myself.

The "God" question is such a parent-stopper for any number of reasons, but foremost among them is that it is a question to which none of us have a real answer. As parents, we are used to having all the answers, at least when it comes to younger children. I haven't hit adolescence yet.

In fact, we ourselves take on some "God-like" qualities in the eyes of our children. We seem able to heal wounds, soothe hurt feelings, fix broken toys, decide exactly when to cross the street and, of course, know the answer to every question. It's a heady experience for any adult.

But when it comes to the *real* God, we blubber. And our children pick up on that. I can set rules in my house such as "no touching the stove" or "always say thank you when someone gives you something" with equanimity, since I know exactly what rule of safety or politeness they are based on, even if my children don't. When all else fails, of course, I can always use that age-old parental prerogative, "Because I said so."

But ask me about God, who or what He (or She) is, and why we observe Shabbat or keep kosher, and I have not necessarily reconciled these questions even for myself. Observance is often based on faith, and faith is a highly personal thing, tricky to convey even to adults.

How I answer my child's questions about God will reveal less about God and more about me, about my own belief system, about how I ponder the imponderable. As Jews, ironically, we are not often called upon to contemplate God. We are taught that we can observe the commandments without necessarily understanding them or understanding God. The traditional answer to why we observe Shabbat or keep kosher is sort of like that same parental standby: "Because God said so."

And so, it was good for my son to prod me to think about God. In trying to discuss God on a four-year-old level, I found myself rediscovering the benevolent God of my own childhood, the divine Friend I had invented for myself who lived up in the sky and looked just like the painting of the holy-looking man wrapped in tallit and tefillin that hung in our dining room.

I tried to encourage my son to look out his window at night, before he went to sleep, and imagine a great and wonderful Being busy supervising the world. That Being could take whatever shape his own mind and heart imagined. I told him about my own "conversations" with this Almighty from my own childhood bedroom.

I thought I was waxing rather eloquently on the topic when I paused to look for his reaction. "But Mama, you still didn't tell me WHAT God is," he exclaimed, clearly exasperated.

I then responded the way any thoughtful parent would in this kind of situation: I told him to go ask his father.

My Own December Dilemma

December 1996

The "holiday season" is upon us and we have come to that time of year when intermarried couples, as well as many other Jewish families in America, face what the experts call the "December dilemma." This dilemma is created by the confluence of Christmas and Chanukah, when families who adhere to both Christianity and Judaism must make all sorts of difficult decisions regarding how to celebrate two major holidays that fall right on top of each other. Even many Jewish families find it difficult to maintain a sense of identity in the face of the annual Christmas barrage.

In my own home, where our Jewish identity runs pretty strong, we face a different kind of December dilemma, although one that is no less related to Christmas. The dilemma we face, for lack of a better term, is what I would call the "Christmastization" of Chanukah.

Now I don't want to sound like a Scrooge and I also don't want to sound like Abe Lincoln recalling my log cabin days, but when I was a kid, all my brother and I got for Chanukah was some Chanukah *gelt* — which amounted to a total of eight cents apiece for the entire holiday. As we got a little older and a little wiser, we upped the ante to a dollar a night, and by the time we were sophisticated young adults, we were shaking my parents down for one nice gift for the holiday.

Here we are, not that many decades later, and I am led to understand that my children will expect no less than a present per night from their parents. This, of course, does not include the gifts from the grandparents, aunts, uncles, and anyone else we might run into during the course of the holiday. Luckily, my children are not yet old enough to realize that this is what they should expect.

I have always thought Christmas, at least as it is celebrated in America today, an enchanting, heartwarming holiday. But I have also been relieved that as a Jew, I did not have to get caught up in the shopping frenzy that seems to consume this country every year between the end of November and the end of December.

But here we seem to be, caught in the same gift-giving cycle as our Christian neighbors. We've even co-opted their slogans. I get flyers to come to a Chanukah fair to "do your Chanukah shopping early"; I get direct-mail marketing aimed at helping me get the gifts I need for everybody on my "Chanukah gift list"; and I am suddenly noticing Chanukah cards in the stationery store, to reach out to my loved ones at this special time of year.

Let's face it, Chanukah was never historically seen as a "major" holiday in the Jewish canon. And even if it were, presents do not form an integral part of most Jewish holidays. We just finished Sukkot — a holiday, unlike Chanukah, that is mentioned in the Bible — and never once did it occur to anyone I know to offer their kids a Sukkot present.

It's not that giving gifts at Chanukah is entirely new or in any way wrong. The tradition goes back at least as far as the term "Chanukah *gelt*." It is really more a question of degree. Christmas was as pervasive when I was a kid as it is now. Something else has changed in the interim.

When we got our penny a night as kids, it was only after the candles were lit, the *brachot* were recited by every member of the family, the latkes were made, and at least one game of dreidel was played.

Now, with both parents working, sometimes crazy hours, there are nights when my husband can't make it home in time for candle-lighting with the kids. On a weekday, I am hard-pressed to find the time to make latkes. And there certainly isn't much time for all of us to sit around and play dreidel.

The presents we lavish on our children are, at least in part, a substitute for the time we don't spend with them. How many times have I shopped for toys that the kids could play with by themselves, that would occupy them while I tended to some other chore?

This, of course, has nothing to do with either Christmas or Chanukah. The December dilemma is, in some ways, the dilemma of how we live our lives. It is the dilemma of time, the dilemma of conflicting priorities, the dilemma not so much of established religion, but of what we actually worship.

Now, I am not issuing a call for "family values," nor do I wish to return to a supposedly simpler era when dinner was on the table at six and Mom always made the latkes. But this Chanukah, I am trying to make some time.

Turning this toy craze on its head, our community — and I'm sure many others — has a Chanukah toy drive, where gifts are collected for needy children. I took the time this year to bring the kids with me to pick the toys they would donate and together, we went to the home where they were being collected and added them to the growing pile.

We are setting up the menorahs together, learning the *brachot* and songs together — and I even called my mother for her latkes recipe. No, I still won't expect my husband home every night, nor do I anticipate a spirited game of dreidel each evening.

But as I shop for presents, I am looking for things that actually require more than one player. That way, as the saying goes, a little of the Chanukah spirit will last the whole year through.

A Women's Room

March 1997

Let's face it: I don't get out much. I have three young children. I work out of my house. My husband keeps late hours at the office. I don't see any of the above-mentioned nearly enough, so when I do go out, it is usually with one of them.

For me to leave the house by myself, not for purposes of career or family, but just to do something I might enjoy — well, let's just say it better be really worth my while; it upsets everybody's schedules too much for me to take such an excursion lightly.

I am not really complaining. I figure I am not alone in this; most women in my station of life are in a similar boat.

And so it was that several weeks ago, I got it into my head to attend a lecture given by Dr. Avivah Zornberg, a noted biblical scholar from Jerusalem. I had to plan in advance; spontaneity does not work well in my life these days. I asked my babysitter to stay late and my husband to come home early, and off I went. I expected to find maybe a few dozen women there from my community, who thought it was worth the hassle just to hear a lecture on a particular passage in Genesis.

I must say that I was more than a little impressed when I entered the building and found a couple hundred women standing in line to get in to the lecture. The hall was packed. Something is going on here, I thought. This scholar is tapping into some quest, some thirst, some desire on the part of these women.

If this impressed me, what took place several weeks later at the Grand Hyatt in Manhattan astounded me. I attended the first International Conference on Feminism and Orthodoxy.

I stood in the grand ballroom of the Grand Hyatt — and when I say "stood," I mean "stood," because there were no seats to be had — surrounded by nearly a thousand women (and a smattering of men), listening to lectures, learning Torah, debating points of *halachah*, and praying together.

All these women had at least a dozen different things they could have been doing over the course of that holiday weekend. I met people who had come from as far away as Seattle, Miami, and Denver. These are women who take their religion seriously. They do not want to reject their heritage; they are trying to find their own way within it. As a group, they cannot easily be dismissed.

I am smiling as I write these words because there are those who attended each of these events — Dr. Zornberg's lecture and the feminism conference—who probably would not appreciate even being written about in the same column. And perhaps some of these women do represent different streams of thought when it comes to how far "women's issues" in Orthodoxy should be taken.

But ladies, let's get real. These are nuances. What is going on today among observant Jewish women is nothing short of momentous. Women, from all parts of the spectrum, are learning Torah — in large numbers, over long periods of time, and with deep levels of commitment. It is as simple and as powerful and as unprecedented as that.

With this knowledge, no doubt, will come other changes — be they in prayer, in religious divorce, or in life-cycle events. But it is the learning — and the learning together, as women — that has already changed us.

I had the opportunity recently to speak with a woman from a right-wing Orthodox neighborhood in Brooklyn who told me how much "courage" it would take in her community to set up a room — "a reading room, with babysitting and food provided" — where women could just sit and learn. I felt like inviting her to the dozens of such rooms that are thriving around the world. Still, it was striking that this was something she and others in her community dream about.

We are all part of a continuum. What takes courage in this woman's community is taken for granted in mine. What takes courage in my own more "modern" world — well, sometimes it may take courage to just leave the husband and kids for an evening to go to a lecture; sometimes it takes courage to join 1,000 women at a conference to engage in issues they all deal with every day but so rarely get a chance to discuss.

It always takes courage to fulfill your potential, and as a group, observant Jewish women are finally starting to do just that.

They will not find one easy path to walk down; in fact, I hope they don't. Generations of men have taught us that learning Torah has always led to differing opinions, different schools of thought — all within the framework of civil discourse, mutual respect, and a shared love of Torah.

The door has been opened. We have stepped inside. And we are now, separately and together, trying to find a room of our own.

The More One Tells the Story

April 1997

I know what the calendar says, but it matters not: in my home, Passover is well under way.

It began a few weeks ago, when I made a wrong turn in my local supermarket and stumbled into...dum da dum dum...the Pesach Zone. There they were — in mid-March — the matzah, the macaroons, the mixes made out of potato starch or matzah meal. I fled from the aisle as fast as I could, but I knew: I could run, but I could not hide.

Having recovered from the initial shock, preparations for the holiday are now picking up steam. My family follows me in dread as I move from room to room, cleaning each one and then declaring it off-limits to further invasion by *chametz* particles. I have, by now, revisited the Passover aisle and actually made purchases from it. The menu for the seders and the rest of the holiday is beginning to take shape and I am checking my inventory of dishes and pots and pans to determine if I need anything new this year.

I may sound as if I've been making Passover at my home for years. In truth, I've only done it twice before. But I had years of training watching my mother prepare for the holiday. As I got older, and so did she, I took on an increasingly larger role in making Pesach, until finally, I "retired" her from active duty, absconded with all her dishes (right down to her kosher-for-Passover Cuisinart), and moved Passover to my house. My brother and I now take turns hosting the family.

It was not easy for my mother to part with her dishes. Like so many other traditions associated with the holiday, these dishes had taken on a life of their own. They had become as integral to our family's celebration of Passover as any seder ritual.

I remember, as a child, helping my mother unpack those dishes from the bags and boxes in which they were stored year-round. We would take the dishes out, wipe them off with care and place them in their appointed Passover spots. They would signal a renewal, a sense at once of freshness and return. They were different from our regular dishes, yet they were the same as last year's Pesach dishes and the year before that, and so on.

Pesach is like that in many ways. It is so different from the rest of the year, but within families, traditions build up from year to year that make the holiday familiar and consistent. No two families seem to celebrate the seder in exactly the same way, despite the uniform text (which is why, after almost ten years, my husband and I still can't agree on what vegetable constitutes "*karpas*").

In my family, there was one seder tradition that became sacred. It came at the point in the Haggadah when it says that in each generation, it is incumbent upon every person to feel as if he (or she) had personally left Egypt.

It was at this point every year — and for most of my youth, the only time all year — that my father would stop, look up from the text, and open the gates to his past for just a brief moment. His voice cracking, his eyes fixed on some distant point, he would share with us one story, one memory, one reflection from his experiences during the Holocaust. And that was all.

For years, none of the family or friends gathered around the table dared to ask questions or pursue the topic. I know for myself that I was too afraid. After a long silence we returned to the text, richer and sadder for this glimpse into my father's own Egypt.

Years have passed, the floodgates have opened, and like so many other Holocaust survivors, my father has broken his silence and has told a fuller version of his experiences. But our seder tradition continues. This, after all, is the making of memory, the making of our personal and communal history, the making of ritual.

The whole point of the Haggadah is the telling, and re-telling, of a story that we all already know. Even if all of us were all scholars, if all of us were knowledgeable and wise, we would still be commanded to tell the story of how we left Egypt — this is what the Haggadah tells us. "And the more one tells the story, the more praiseworthy it is," the Haggadah says.

We tell these stories — of ancient Egypt and more recent Germany, and of our redemption from each — so that our children will learn, and so that we, ourselves, will never, never forget.

A happy Passover to all.

The Mourning Never Stops

May 1997

During this past year, I have watched three mothers bury their children.

The circumstances of the children's deaths could not have been more different. Sara Duker, a 22-year-old recent college graduate, was killed by a terrorist's bomb on a bus in Jerusalem in February 1996. Maidi Katz, a 34-year-old lawyer and Jewish scholar living in New York, took her own life in November. And Coby Levi, a three-and-a-half-year-old boy from Teaneck, died in January after a long and tortuous battle with cancer.

Despite the vastly different circumstances, these deaths had in common the fact that they reversed the natural order of things. Parents should never have to bury their children.

I don't think a day goes by when I am not reminded, in one way or another, of one or more of these lost children and their parents. Sara Duker's mother and sisters live on my block. Maidi Katz was my college roommate and dear friend. And Coby Levi's parents are friends of ours; our children are all about the same ages.

I choose to write about these individuals now because Yom Hashoah is approaching. And the deaths of children reverberate.

In a year in which Madeleine Albright was forced out of the closet and the Swiss banks are finally owning up to their not-exactly neutral status, I have begun to realize that the fall-out from the Holocaust is greater than I could have ever imagined. It is immense. More than fifty years after the events themselves, the Shoah just won't seem to go away. It refuses to be consigned to history.

I saw it for myself over Passover, which just ended. There was my father, a Holocaust survivor now in his 70s, sitting at the head of the seder table, with his now sizeable family all around — his wife, his two children, their spouses, and his six healthy, rambunctious grandchildren, all under the age of seven. There were his oldest grandchildren singing all the Pesach songs they had learned in school, asking the Four Questions, hiding the afikomen — it was plenty to make a grandparent proud.

And yet, the first seder night is the anniversary of the start of the Warsaw Ghetto Uprising. And in speaking about it, and remembering the heroes who fell during that brave, fiery moment, my father began to weep. He could not continue. "The mourning never stops," said my mother, through her own tears. "It takes a toll on a person to never stop mourning for 50 years."

I used to think, until this year, that a family scene such as the one at the seder table was a sign that, somehow, in the end, we had "won." That life had gone on. That the survivors had picked up the pieces, married, had children, and now grandchildren, and had ensured the continuity of the Jewish people. I thought that each Jewish child born today is a *"nechamah,"* a comfort for a child lost in the Shoah.

But I learned, through the seemingly unrelated events of this past year, through the deaths of individual children, that this *nechamah* can only go so far. The children who died this past year were isolated cases, not victims of mass genocide. In each agonizing case, I could see and get at least some taste of the immense grief and unspeakable tragedy that each death involved.

And now, I have come to understand, as a mother and as one who has watched other mothers bury their children: A child lost is a child lost. He or she is irreplaceable.

On this Yom Hashoah, I will know that we did not "win." We have continued, we have succeeded in replenishing the Jewish people. We have the State of Israel and Jewish communities thriving in all parts of the world. But no matter how many other children are born, the ones who are gone are gone forever. In that sense, we have lost so very, very much.

Summertime

July 1997

Summertime and the livin's easy.... Ha!

My kids' days are long and lazy and wet and unstructured. Mine keep up the pace they've adhered to all year long — demanding, stressful, and carefully structured.

We live in a society obsessed with time, and in the summer months, this obsession can seem particularly cruel and unnatural. For working parents, this obsession borders on the fanatical.

Every parcel of the day is allotted for a particular task, be it at work or at home. There is little "give" time, where activities can stretch to take a little longer than planned or delays can be accounted for and not cause distress.

And yet my children's summer does beckon. Everybody's bedtime is later, since no one has to get up for school the next day. As such, our evenings together are longer. We are more prone to being outdoors, to stopping in at neighbors' homes unannounced, to buying ice cream on a whim. Time seems a bit more fluid, less rigid.

The slightly extra time accentuates for me something that my mother spelled out to me years ago, in the first crazy weeks after the birth of my first child. I plaintively asked my mother how I was ever going to figure out what the baby wanted when he cried, or, even better, how to anticipate what the baby would want before he started crying.

Debunking the "quality time" myth in one fell swoop, my mother assured me that all I needed was time. The more time I would spend with the baby, she explained, the more easily

I would come to understand how to meet his needs and even make him smile. The more time I would spend with him, the more time I would want to spend with him. I learned, as my children grew, that this is even more true as they get older.

When I have three hours to spend with my three children every night after I finish work, I find myself keeping to a tight schedule, impatient with any child who stays too long in the bathtub, annoyed when I have to read more than one book at bedtime, relieved when I get them all into bed and can finally get on to do what I need to do in the evening.

But when I spend a long Sunday at the beach or at a museum or in the park with my kids, I don't want the day to end. I have time for everyone, I enjoy all their foibles, and I let the day take us where it will, without always glancing at my watch. My kids, in turn, seem to make the time for me, as well.

Of course, not every Sunday can work that way. Sunday is often a day of planned activities or running errands or even, sometimes, working.

And that is why God created Shabbat. Shabbat transcends time. No matter how busy the week, no matter how many things still remain to get done, Shabbat comes and all the workaday demands stand still. They are frozen in time until 25 hours later, when Shabbat ends.

To me, the essence of Shabbat can be felt in its last few hours, particularly during the long *Shabbatot* of the summer months. You know that soon, within a few hours, your life will resume where you left it Friday afternoon. The dishes will have to be washed, the bills will have to be paid, phone calls will have to be returned. If you're lucky, you'll get in a movie.

But for now, as if held back by some unseen hand, you do none of this. Deliciously, you just play with the baby or watch the show the older kids are putting on, or even, if you're lucky, curl up with the book you never get to read.

There is a lot more to Shabbat, of course. And every Jew will celebrate Shabbat as he or she thinks is most fitting. But, if nothing else, Shabbat is about time and about the sanctity of time. We make Kiddush Friday night to sanctify the Shabbat that has just begun. We will go to synagogue, eat good meals, visit with friends, and learn some Torah.

But most of all, we will allow ourselves to worship God and not time. We will allow ourselves to just be, rather than let time dictate to us. In our current time-starved world, Shabbat is the Jewish family's ace in the hole. It is quantity time and quality time all rolled into one.

If Shabbat is our holiest day, and we consecrate it by consecrating time, then time must be one of our most sacred commodities. Let us not always use it "efficiently" or "productively." Let us use it well.

A Wish for the New Year

October 1997

I have a son. He is my second-born, and he is about to turn four this month. I suspect that perhaps every family has a child like this one.

This is the one who most beguiles. He can, in turn, enchant and exasperate, delight and infuriate. He is exuberant, often rambunctious, and yet at times, painfully shy and sweet. This is the one with the perennial twinkle in the eye, where you're never quite sure if it is mischief or sheer joy that makes it shine.

This is the child who literally wakes up in the morning singing. He then sneaks into his baby sister's room, pokes his hand through the slats of the crib, and wakes her up so she can join him. Listening from your bedroom, you don't know whether to smile at the sweetness of the whole thing or wring his neck because now the baby is up and that means you have to get out of bed.

This is the child who can spend minutes repeatedly jumping off an increasingly higher and higher ledge, refusing any help, climbing back up after every jump, determined to make the next one. Then, suddenly, without warning, he realizes he probably should be frightened. He bursts into tears, dissolves into a complete temper tantrum, and demands that you carry him for the next five blocks.

This is the child who loves nothing more than to be hugged and kissed, who tackles his father at the door when the latter comes home from work, and laughs out loud as he wrestles with his big brother. But when he is sad or down, and you just want to hold him tight, he squirms out of your embrace and runs off to his room to be alone.

He is different from me, more different than my other children are. He is a daredevil in the playground, while I was always the scaredy-cat. He is visual — loving to paint, and build and dress up — while I am more the wordsmith. We go together to the exhibit on knights and armor at the Metropolitan Museum of Art: I see history and grandeur; he sees swords and horses and "scary masks," all of which charm him to no end.

My son and I, as you might guess, have had our moments.

But lately, as I have learned to let him lead, rather than make him follow, we have had some exquisite moments. And I write this about him now, as the New Year begins, because I want to share one such point in time.

It happened late in the summer, while we were on vacation. We were staying on a farm with my brother-in-law and his family, and everyone decided to take a walk on Shabbat afternoon. Everyone, that is, except my second son, who stood his ground and refused to follow the pack.

So he and I stayed on the farm, and I asked him what he wanted to do instead. Without saying a word, he led me to the pen where the turkeys and roosters were kept and pointed inside. I somewhat reluctantly opened the fence for him, and he ran in.

For more than an hour, my son ran around that chicken coop, chasing the birds, feeding them, talking to them, singing, dancing. He was thoroughly happy, wondrously joyous. He himself was like a bird let loose to fly.

I watched my son in awe. And while I watched, I felt all my cares slip away. With him, there, for that hour, there was no past, no future, only the present. There were no pressures, no places I had to go to, no people I had to see. There was only this — a beautiful Shabbat afternoon, the roosters running around, and my gorgeous son.

There is a passage that we recite on Rosh Hashanah that I have always loved but never fully understood until this son of mine entered my life. We say it in the Musaf service, when we ask God to have mercy on us, as He has told us in the past that He would.

The prayer book cites a verse in Jeremiah, where the prophet assures the Jewish people that God would take pity on them, the way a father does with his child. Jeremiah quotes God referring to his beloved son as a *"yeled sha'ashuim"* —a playful child, a delightful child. This describes all our children on some level, but for me, most specifically, it epitomizes my son.

"Whenever I speak of him, I remember him fondly. Therefore, I yearn for him, and I will have mercy on him, says the Lord."

My wish for this New Year is that we can all have at least one hour such as the one I spent with my son on that farm: an hour of peace, an hour of plenitude, an hour of health and hope, an hour of thanking God for all that is before us. May the year be filled with many such hours, in our own lives and for all the Jewish people.

Me And My *Chavrusa*

November 1997

This month marks the 12th anniversary of a relationship in my life that predates my marriage, children, and many friendships. It is a relationship that has spanned not only years, but also many miles, since the other person has lived in Tokyo, Singapore, Hong Kong, and Australia for parts of the time that we have known each other. (I, alas, have moved only to New Jersey).

This relationship is with my *chavrusa*, or learning partner, and we have been practicing the time-honored art of learning Talmud together since shortly after we finished graduate school. True to the image that *"chavrusa"* conjures up, when we learn together each week, we read from the text in a sing-song voice, use our hands while we speak, and get worked up over hair-splitting distinctions in Jewish law.

But ours is a truly modern *chavrusa*. When we were young and single, we used to learn after midnight since that's when I got off work in my first journalism job. When Judy went to Tokyo for the Wall Street firm she works for, we switched our in-person learning to the phone line — Sundays, 10 p.m. her time, 9 a.m. my time. This set-up remained for the four years she spent in the Far East and Down Under; the only thing that changed was the time zone.

Now, we're in the same country, but on different sides of the Hudson River, and we juggle our learning schedule around jobs, husbands, and kids.

When we learn Sunday evenings, the kids are in bed, the weekend is coming to a close, and we pause for an hour or two before the work-week sets in. Often in my sweatpants, I settle into a chair in the living room, tractate in hand, while she does the same on her end, and we begin our phone calls the way I suspect *chavrusas* have done from time immemorial: we catch up on each other's news and only then plunge into the text.

Our *chavrusa* is modern in a different sense, as well. For Judy and I are women, of course, and in choosing to learn together as we do, we have embraced a tradition that never really imagined us. The mandate to learn, which runs so deep in the Jewish experience, was never addressed to women. "And ye shall teach them your sons," the Torah says (Deuteronomy 11:19). It is the Talmud itself that adds (Kedushin 29b): "But not your daughters." It is not for me to try to elucidate the myriad of interpretations of this talmudic phrase and others like it; suffice it to say that the rabbinic texts have not been kind to the notion of women entering their hallowed lines.

This has not made them less of a pull for Judy and me and countless numbers of other women. And so, of course, the question: Why? Why do we do this? Why, no matter what our life circumstances, do we keep coming back to our *chavrusa*?

I have no simple answer. I suspect we keep at it for much the same reasons that Jews have kept at it for hundreds of years. As a difficult, seemingly arcane text, the Talmud offers endless opportunity for interpretation, even creativity.

Making your way through the Talmud is an incredible intellectual adventure; you follow the rabbis step by step, you carry each argument to its logical conclusion, you learn to appreciate how our religious practice was built from the foundations of the Torah. Eventually, you actually get a kick out of figuring out under what circumstances a baby boy can or cannot be circumcised on Shabbat, or why the shofar is sounded exactly 100 times on Rosh Hashanah.

And then there is the more personal side, the aspect of learning that connects me to my own heritage. Learning is the one practice that seems to anchor me most to the world of my grandparents, a world that I never knew. Proudly, my mother and father each refer to their own fathers as *talmidei chachamim*, learned men — men who studied in some of the finest yeshivas in prewar Europe, men for whom learning was the highest pursuit, valued above all else.

What would these pious men have made of their granddaughter? I would not be so presumptuous as to answer this question with any certainty. But I can entertain my own hopes.

I like to think that when my *chavrusa* and I pore over the texts my grandparents held so dear, I am in some way connecting with them, in substance if not in style. I like to think that I am drawing from the same well — the well that gave them their strength and our religion its endurance. Now that I have children, I am hoping they go to that same well, too.

We are all uttering the same words; each in our own voice.

Fellow Travellers for the Season

December 1998

So there I was at the Dallas-Ft. Worth International Airport — don't ask — with about an hour and a half to kill before my flight back to New York. I am by no means a well seasoned traveler, and though I had been away only two days, I couldn't wait to get home. I ended up spending most of my time buying Dallas Cowboys paraphernalia for my kids and hunting for some food, since I had failed to order kosher food for the trip home.

Finally, I decided it was time to find my gate. I walked down a seemingly endless corridor, schlepping my bags, looking for my gate. I got about two-thirds of the way down the aisle when, suddenly, I knew I had arrived at the right place: there, as if a mirage in the midst of the Dallas desert, a large hasidic family was camped out, waiting for the flight to New York.

I felt this sudden urge to rush over and embrace them like long-lost relatives, to share with one another the travails of being so far from our respective shtetls in the New York metropolitan area (I was also tempted to ask them for some food, since they were naturally well-stocked for the journey).

But, alas, short of going over to them and introducing myself, I had no way to signal to them that we were — literally — fellow travelers, members of the same tribe, "*lantsmen*." And what if I had gone over to them? Would they have felt a true kinship toward me? I have opted to live a life in which my Jewish observance is not obvious to the naked eye. I wear no outward sign of my Jewishness, let alone of my religious commitment.

This is my choice, of course, and most of the time I am quite comfortable with it. In fact, I admit, it has served me well in the workplace and other settings. But there are times, and that moment in Dallas was one of them, when I almost envy the hasidim their *bekeshes* (the long coats many of the men wear) and their *sheitels* (the wigs worn by the married women).

There they were, out in the Wild West, loudly, confidently, and yet unself-consciously proclaiming their Jewishness. Sure, I blended in with the crowd, I didn't stick out, no one stared at me. But I was the one who felt alone and isolated, out of my element.

They, on the other hand, could create a sense of community almost instantly. Any Jew happening by would immediately feel a connection. Had another hasid or recognizably Jewish person come along, they would have been breaking bread together within minutes.

I think about this chance encounter as we head into the "holiday season" — a term, which, while meant to be inclusive, is really just a euphemism for the Christmas season. In an era of unprecedented comfort and security for Diaspora Jews, December is probably the only time of year when we really notice our separateness.

For those of us who blend almost seamlessly into the American fabric most of the time, December reminds us of the limits to this approach. Sure, we can buy our Chanukah presents as aggressively as they buy their Christmas gifts, we can incorporate the gift-giving almost too centrally into our holiday, we can even get into the "Christmas spirit" — if that is defined in its most charitable sense.

But most Jews — though certainly not all — stop short of actually celebrating Christmas. This, as opposed to say, Thanksgiving, where many Jews partake as heartily as their

Christian neighbors. Christmas is where we don't fade into the woodwork, we don't go unnoticed, we do stick out.

And maybe that's a healthy thing, a good thing for the Jewish people. Like the hasidim I spied at the Dallas airport, you can spot a Jew at Christmastime a mile away. They're the ones at the movies or the Chinese restaurants, or, in more recent years, they're the ones snaking around the block to get into the Jewish Museum on Christmas Day or joining in days of learning at various synagogues and institutions in and around the city.

And at a time when we Jews are caught up in all our differences and the gaps that lie between each of our little groups, Christmas is as good a time as any to remind ourselves of what binds us together. It is a time to remember that the things that unite us are far greater and more fundamental than those that divide us.

So, enjoy having the kids home from school, enjoy having a lighter schedule at work, have a wonderful Chanukah, and go take in a good exhibit at the museum. Make the most of the season.

On Passover, the Tale is in the Telling

April 1998

It's that time of the year again, and preparations for Passover are in full fury at my home.

I have descended, along with every other Jew in my community, on my local supermarket, clearing its Pesach aisle out before the last snowfall. I have stocked up on the fake Cheerios, the crumbly chocolate chip cookies, and the virtual noodles — the barebone necessities upon which my kids will survive for the duration of the holiday.

I have turned my house inside out, become a demon about restricted chometz zones, and transformed my kitchen into a sea of silver foil that lines every shelf and counter space available.

While much has been written and said over the years (mostly by men) about the "spiritual cleansing" that is a byproduct of the arduous physical cleaning for Pesach, I find little comfort in metaphor while scrubbing my refrigerator at 1 o'clock in the morning.

But there are definitely parts of the process that I do enjoy. This coming week, for example, I am expecting the following holiday inventory to arrive in my home: two seder plates, two cups of Elijah, two matzah covers, one afikomen bag, and one Haggadah.

Together, these items are valued at well over ten thousand dollars, since that is how much we pay in tuition for our two young artisans to make these handcrafted seder ornaments. And let's not forget, these items come on top of similar brought home last year and the year before that, jewels that are stashed away at the end of each holiday to be stored until the following year.

And oh, the productions that accompany the presentation of these projects! The solemnity, the excitement with which my kids unveil each treasure is more precious to me than the items themselves. Each product comes with a story — how it was made, which teacher supervised and what purpose its serves on the holiday.

What is the etiquette in the matter of preserving these artifacts? Clearly, this year's fashions are the ones we must use during this year's seders. But no self-respecting parent can then discard the seder plates of yesteryear, now can they? For how many years does this go on? My mother still uses the Haggadah covers I made when I was six. Is this extreme?

Of course, the question of how long and under what conditions to save your children's projects is not unique to Passover. My oldest is still only in kindergarten and my house is already overrun with projects ranging from elaborate representations of the alphabet to a family tree in honor of Tu B'Shevat. All sorts of more non-descript items come home on a weekly basis. My refrigerator door is only so big.

But Pesach, somehow, is in a category by itself. At the end of the holiday, everything is packed away, from the finest crystal to the most humble afikomen bag. When you unpack these same items the following year, you unpack your memories.

Each one of my dishes, most of them given to me by my mother, holds within it memories of Pesachs past. Each pot, it seems, has its own story to tell. And now, so do my children's home-made Elijah cups. When so many of us come from families that started out with nothing in this country, these are our family heirlooms.

And this, of course, is what Passover is all about. It's about stories and memories and going over the same material, over and over again. It's about making the past come to life, through the retelling of a tale, using the visual props that constitute our seder centerpieces.

We always say that the telling of the Exodus story each year is for the sake of the children, so that they shall know our history. And all the unusual and different objects that we use at the seder are to keep the children awake and sustain their interest.

But I have discovered a little secret about this educational process. It actually works both ways. "You wanna hear something, Mama?" my four-year-old son asks me, as he unveils the vividly green cardboard frog that he made in school.

He then proceeds to tell me, wide-eyed, the most amazing thing about frogs jumping around in Pharoah's bed. He shares this story with me in a rush, like a hot news item, letting me in on his discovery, confident that I could never have heard of such a thing before.

And, in a way, I never have. I have never heard his version of the story. When he tells it to me, it is fresh, it is spontaneous, and it is interpreted by him. The Haggadah tells us that no matter how well we think we know the story of the Exodus, it is incumbent upon us to recite it every year and to see ourselves as if we too were redeemed from Egypt.

When we hear the story told to us by our children, no matter how simply or how fantastically, it really is as if we have never heard it before. And when our children have internalized our history and are able to tell it back to us anew — this truly is redemption.

Happy Birthday, Israel

May 1998

If I forget thee, O Jerusalem...

A phrase seared into the history of the Jewish people and incorporated into our every tradition and ritual. Above every *simcha* and every joy, we remember our beloved crown jewel, Jerusalem.

And in times of true sorrow, or true joy, I do not forget Zion. Even wonderful family times, such as our recent celebration of Passover, bring Israel and our ancient ties to it right to the forefront of my very soul.

But my sins I do confess today. I have, regretfully, been forgetting. Or perhaps, more specifically, I find the ties loosening, I find Jerusalem and Israel being pushed further back in my head, away from the hustle and bustle of my current existence.

My personal sense of Judaism has always been intimately tied up with Israel. As strong as my commitment has always been to Shabbat, *kashrut*, and a host of other religious practices not related to place, I have long felt that Jewish life as it is lived in the Diaspora in the latter half of the 20th century is almost by definition derivative.

We are not quite in Israel, but our modern-day observance is completely wrapped up in the existence of Israel. Even leaders of the secular Jewish community believe that sending American Jewish youngsters to Israel for a summer or a year will somehow instil in them enough Jewish identity to last a lifetime.

And in terms of religious identity, I do not doubt any Jew's fervor, including my own, when we sing so passionately at the end of the seder, "Next year in Jerusalem." But given the very real and vibrant existence of Jerusalem in our day, and the means that almost all of us have to get there if we wanted to, how we can we recite that line without it sounding just a bit hollow?

I used to wrestle with these questions all the time, and failed to come up with satisfying, meaningful answers. My family is here, my vocation is here, I can contribute to the Jewish community here, too. These have been my rationalizations. I don't know exactly when my wrestling stopped and my life just took over, but I do know that I have largely stopped wrestling.

Now, it is not so much that I don't live there, although that is obviously a large part of it — it is that I don't think a lot about Israel and all the challenges it poses anymore. My focus is on my family, my community, my own little corner of Jewish life. I know this may violate the first tenet of American Judaism, but when I pick up *The New York Times* every morning, I don't always read the article about Israel first.

With this "forgetting" of Jerusalem comes a true loss in my life — a loss not only of my Zionist fervor, but a loss of focus and a loss of idealism. I feel that I, along with many other Jews of my generation, both in Israel and outside it, have lost our way when it comes to Israel.

It is not as pristine as it once was, and, neither, of course, are we. We are no longer quite sure what to make of Israel, and if we are not living there, what to make of it in our lives.

And so I welcome all this fuss about Israel's 50th. I welcome the flurry of activity at my kids' schools, the local and international celebrations, the commemorative series in *The New York Times*, the public reflections of the last remaining pioneers. It has taken all this to jolt me awake from my stupor and remind me — in case I'd forgotten — of the wondrous miracle that is Israel.

Against all odds, a nation was created in 1948 and is still going strong 50 years later — a nation born from the ashes of the Holocaust and from the struggles and sacrifices of the early settlers. This reminds me of my faith, and I welcome that, too.

The marvelously thriving and deeply conflicted country that we are sometimes too quick to criticize today is still built on this solid foundation. It remains for us as a people and for many of us individually the well from which we draw sustenance and try to replenish as best as we can.

This is an imperfect relationship, but it is at least an ongoing one. My goal is to ensure that it is carried on well into my children's and grandchildren's generations, and beyond. We are nowhere without this blessed, often tormented, land. That, above all, we must never forget.

As my son kept repeating all week: Happy birthday, Israel.

A Jew is a Jew is a Jew

February 1998

In my home growing up, there were basically two kinds of people in the world: Jews and non-Jews. No other distinctions really mattered.

While this may not have been the most broad-minded approach to the world at large, it seems in retrospect to have been a quaintly liberal one when it comes to the Jewish world.

Today, after all, it is not enough simply to be a Jew. You need a movement to belong to, or at least a defining adjective. It is not even enough to say you are an "observant" Jew, or a "religious" Jew — terms, again, from my youth.

You must be Reform or Reconstructionist or Conservative or Modern Orthodox or Ultra Orthodox. And within each of those movements, you must identify with a particular stream of thought or a particular leader or a particular political view.

I have so far confined my "Home Front" column largely to the home, to topics that unite us, rather than divide us. I have purposely left Jewish politics, both here and abroad, to those steeped in the issues. But Jewish politics have crept up to my front door, and try as I might, I cannot keep them out. I suspect I am not alone.

Everywhere I turn, I am asked for my Jewish identity card — in shul, in my children's schools, in conversation with friends. My husband and I have begun attending a new minyan that meets near our home. One of its attractions to us is that it brings together in prayer Jews from a variety of backgrounds and affiliations. The group does not fit neatly into any one category — a fact that seems automatically to place it under a cloud of suspicion.

And while my husband and I identify ourselves as Orthodox, we were also suspect because we largely supported the Israeli peace process under the late Prime Minister Yitzhak Rabin.

These are not isolated incidents. Events and issues ranging from the upcoming conference on feminism and Orthodoxy to the debate over pluralism in Israel have become political or religious Rorschach tests in the various communities in which we live. How you view them or whether you support them immediately places you firmly in one camp or another.

But this kind of stereotyping and categorizing shortchanges us all. We are each more complex than the institutions or movements to which we belong. We are each more than the sum of our religious or political parts. As people of the book and of the mind, can't we respect these differences in each other?

The vitriol emanating from the top, with religious leaders of all denominations stooping to vilify one another personally, is bound to have an effect on the community level. More and more people I know are feeling forced to take sides and are becoming radicalized in the process. The gray areas are fading fast; the middle is not holding.

I recently had the opportunity to interview a woman in her mid-50s, who told me of her odyssey from a Reform Sunday school upbringing to her current eclectic Orthodox observance.

She described a New York of 20 to 30 years ago, where, in a quest to learn more about Judaism, she would attend lecture series at the 92nd St. Y given by an Orthodox rabbi one week, a Reform rabbi the next. One summer she took off from work to attend a two-month program at the Conservative movement's Jewish Theological Seminary.

As I listened to her, I couldn't help thinking how permeable the boundaries were then. The ideas flowed, the debate was free and open, and the atmosphere was one of honest intellectual and spiritual growth.

We have lost this sense of mutual respect, of an ability to agree to disagree, of a sense that we are all Jews and that ultimately, we are in this together.

Well, I guess I too have become radicalized. And I hereby stake out my ground as a radical moderate, a zealot of Jewry, not of any branch within it. I know I am not alone, but I fear that those caught in the crossfire have remained silent for too long. My basic credo: I don't have to condone how everyone practices their Judaism, but I don't have to condemn, either.

There are many who will disagree with this view and perhaps call it naive, at best. They might argue that there is only one true path and to accept any other is sacrilege. But I am not calling on anyone to compromise on their own beliefs, merely to honor the integrity of others'. Even if you want to save someone's soul, you have to be able to respect it first.

"A Jew is a Jew is a Jew," my mother always says. In my childhood home, this view may have been a fall-out from the Holocaust, when distinctions among Jews didn't matter squat.

But as an adult now, and particularly, as a parent, I have embraced this approach because it seems to me to be the only Jewish thing to do. One of the tenets of our religion, after all, is to "Love Your Neighbor as Yourself." This seems to me the only way to preserve the future of the Jewish people as one people.

One of my highest priorities as a Jewish parent is to raise my children to love and respect Jews and Judaism. I want them to care very, very deeply about their practice and their beliefs — but not at anyone else's expense.

You Can Go Home Again

September 1996

Rosh Hashanah is approaching, and with it, my annual trip to my parents' shul, the shul I grew up in.

The synagogue is literally a shell of its former self. A huge, grand structure, built in the 1920s, it is populated during the year by a small group of mostly elderly men and women. Their children have grown and moved away and the younger people moving into the neighborhood have flocked to different synagogues. It is a far cry from the thriving, bustling synagogue of my youth.

And yet, every year, once a year, the shul comes back to life. It is as if time stands still, or goes in reverse — to a time and a place that are no longer. It used to be the chazzan — a Holocaust survivor who could open the gates of heaven with his mellifluous, plaintive voice — who brought everyone back. Now, he too is gone.

And yet, for reasons I have never fully fathomed, once a year, the children still return to their parents' shul. Some years back, a friend of mine from the synagogue put it succinctly when she explained why she was pushing off her scheduled aliyah date until after Yom Kippur: "For Sukkot, it will be really nice to be in Jerusalem. But for Rosh Hashanah and Yom Kippur, all that matters is what shul you're in. And this is my shul."

Now, when the children come back, they often have grandchildren in tow. The old gym is opened to accommodate all the little ones who cannot sit still through the long Rosh Hashanah services. Adults return to the same seats they have occupied on the High Holy Days for decades, even though there are now huge gaps between the clusters of families. Grown children take the seats once owned by parents who are no longer alive or too ill to make it to services.

It is here, surrounded by the familiar, comforting, albeit peeling walls and ceiling, that I find inspiration for the most poignant services of the year. It is here, in the shul that time forgot, that I mark time's inexorable progress.

The shul is my touchstone, my point of reference. Perhaps the very fact that it seems so unchanged from year to year makes it is easier to measure all the changes that have occurred in its congregants' lives during that time. It is a point of stability in a world where so little stays the same.

As befitting the liturgy, all I need do is look around the shul to see who in the past year has lived and who has died, who has gained an additional grandchild and who has lost a grandparent. I know exactly where everyone is supposed to sit; it is impossible for me not to notice if a familiar face is missing or a new one has appeared.

Since the longtime chazzan passed away, replacements have come and gone. But the congregation, almost in conspiracy against these upstarts, persists in using the melodies bequeathed to it by its former leader. The melodies remind those present of the glory that this shul once was; perhaps, too, they remind them of their own glory years, when they were busy raising families, building up a shul, forging a community. They have much they can reflect on with some satisfaction, not the least of which is that the vast majority of their children have followed in their footsteps and remain committed and observant Jews.

I have dragged my husband, and now my children, back to this shul year after year, despite its melancholy atmosphere. I cannot speak for all my peers who keep returning to their parents' shul, but I know that I have a need each year to be here, to know that my family and I have made it through another year, to know that we are still intact — to know, in fact, that we are continuing to grow.

I have long known that this shul and this tradition of returning will not last forever. There will come a time when my husband and children and I will celebrate Rosh Hashanah — as we do most other holidays by now — in our own home and our own shul. There, we will create our own family traditions that I hope our children will one day cherish.

Each year at my parents' shul has thus become that much more precious. And each year, I say a silent *"Shehecheyanu,"* thanking God that I have not only moved forward during this past year, but I have lived to come back to my past. It is this sanctuary, after all, that at one time heard all my secret prayers, all my heartfelt aspirations that I confessed nowhere else. It is a rare privilege, I have come to realize, to be able to touch base with the repository of one's dreams.

And so, each year I return, to sit next to my mother in the women's section, in the same seats we have sat in for years. I will no doubt complain, as I do each year, that we can't really see the proceedings from our seats. But I know, despite all the empty seats around us, that we will never move.

Over the past few years, my husband has been added to the seat next to my father, and then my first son and then my second. This year, for the first time, I will bring my newborn daughter to shul, to be cooed over by her grandmother and all the other grandmothers around us. And there we will sit, three generations of my family — a rare privilege indeed; and I will lift my voice in the same prayer that I have made every year: Please may we all be together, in this shul, for Rosh Hashanah next year.

L'Shanah Tova Tikatayvu V'Techataymu. May we all be inscribed for a happy, healthy and peaceful New Year.

The Holiday Hangover

October 2002

By the time Simchat Torah rolled around last week, most everyone I know was suffering from what I might call Yontif fatigue. This syndrome is characterized, especially among women, by: a) an overwhelming aversion to the kitchen and all things having to do with food; b) a sense that, while God is great, ritualized prayer can be excessive; c) and a renewed understanding of why you no longer live year-round with your parents and siblings.

If I were on rabbinic Judaism's ritual committee, I would not have clustered together four major holidays within four weeks, but then again, nobody asked me. I suppose maybe if I were a farmer, I'd get into the whole Harvest Festival thing, but as it stands now, there's this great buildup to Rosh Hashanah and Yom Kippur, leaving Sukkot and Simchat Torah as also-rans. Instead of looking forward to the revelry and joy of Simchat Torah, we often end up feeling put upon — another long morning of shul, another meal to cook. Most years, reactions to the holiday season range from, "I lost the month of September" to "I basically told my boss I'd see her in about a month" to "When do I get my Sundays back?"

When the holiday season comes to a close, as it did this week, a collective sigh of relief can be heard from most Jewish households. Finally, we can get back to work. Finally, the kids are back in school. Finally, the kitchen is closed and will not reopen till maybe Thanksgiving. There's a sense of getting back to things, of the year finally being underway, instead of coming along in bits and pieces, only to be interrupted by a different holiday each week. You can finally get things DONE — be it at work, around the house, or with the kids.

But let's face it. There is also a bit of a let-down. Maybe it's because most of the holidays this year were on weekends, or maybe I'm imagining a mood swing this year because of my own health problems, but I sensed among people a bit more of a reluctance to let go of the holidays this year. "It's a nice time of year," a friend said simply.

For all the griping, it is a time of year where the emphasis is on faith, family, and community. We are almost forced, by the strictures of the holidays, to spend time contemplating our deeds and hanging out with friends and family. The weather this year was for the most part glorious, and the simple act of walking over to a friend's house and lingering there for the afternoon constituted almost an act of rebellion against our otherwise insanely busy lives. How indolent, how unproductive, how absolutely refreshing.

Don't get me wrong. I am, by nature, a creature of habit. I crave routine; it is, in fact, one of the things I miss most since having my life turned upside down by cancer. I've written complete odes to the mundane. I like nothing more than the satisfaction of a productive day at the office and an evening of homework, piano lessons, and soccer. One busy but ordinary day followed reliably by the next. I could wish for nothing more.

But sometimes, maybe, I might have missed the back-story. Are days like Shabbat and holidays a distraction from real life — or are they, on some level, the point? Don't we work hard and try to provide the best for our children at least in part so that we can enjoy those quiet moments, those get-togethers with friends and family, those days of communion with a Higher Authority?

Think of the language of our day-to-day. Now that the holidays are over, we get to return to our commitments, our projects, our schedules. Somehow these words do not convey life. They convey the means to an end. They convey a constant clambering up, trying to reach some kind of plateau, some sense of accomplishment. Maybe on the holidays, which take us out of our normal existence, we get a taste of what that plateau might feel like. It's the same feeling we can get on Shabbat, but it permeates for a month, instead of a day.

And so, as we re-enter our real lives, and get caught up in our daily routines, maybe we can take a piece of the holiday spirit with us — the spirit of quiet reflection, and connectedness with family and community. Maybe we can pause to make sure that our busyness does not get in the way of our priorities, that our schedules do not obscure real meaning, that our commitments do not prevent us from spending time with those people and ideals to which we are truly committed.

And just remember — Chanukah comes early this year…

In Praise of Heroes

February 2000

The woman in the elevator saw me reading the nametag on her lapel. Helpfully, she told me her name and added immediately, "I was born in the Bergen-Belsen DP camp. My parents are from..." and she named two towns in Eastern Europe that I had never heard of.

At first, I was taken aback by this outpouring. It was less an introduction, in the conventional sense, than a reaching out, an attempt at connection. So it was throughout the conference, "Life Reborn: Jewish Displaced Persons 1945-1951," that I attended last month. It was sponsored by the U.S. Holocaust Memorial Museum.

There, in the almost surreal setting of a Marriott hotel in Washington, D.C., survivors of the worst conflagration of the last century — and their children — gathered together to examine how they managed to build new lives from the ruins of the Holocaust. They came to listen to each other, to veterans of the Allied forces who helped liberate them and to historians who tried to put the whole experience in scholarly perspective.

But mostly, I think, they came to connect. The survivors themselves, now mostly in their 70s and 80s, came to a place where their suffering and pain could be relieved for a while, if only because it could be shared and thus confirmed. And their children — many of them born in the DP camps themselves — came also to meet others like themselves, who share the burden and the privilege of serving as living testaments to the fact that their parents, against all odds, chose life over despair.

The period in question, unlike the Holocaust itself, is relatively little studied and little discussed. And yet, especially for the children of survivors, it holds more keys to understanding our parents than their horrific wartime experiences. The Holocaust was done to our parents; in the postwar period, they were the ones who were doing. This is when they were able to resume their humanity, to make choices, to help decide their destiny.

The central question of this period, as put by Menachem Rosensaft, founding chairman of the International Network of Children of Jewish Holocaust Survivors, who was himself born in a DP camp, was this: "What happened to the victims when they stopped being victims?"

What happened was nothing short of a miracle. I never knew before the extent to which life flourished in the DP camps. Every camp had its own governing committee, its own newspapers, its own schools, and its own share of weddings. In 1946-1947, the camps boasted the highest birth rate in the world. From these camps emerged the mass illegal immigration to Palestine, providing perhaps the single most dramatic piece of evidence that the survivors had chosen to build a future rather than succumb to the past.

And so I came to this conference to hear the answer to Rosensaft's question from my own father, who spoke at one of the sessions. I had never been to one of these conferences before. It was part history lesson and part group therapy. On some level, I, and most of the 800 people there, felt a level of comfort in this environment that we may never feel in our daily lives. We were among our own kind, with everyone carrying around similar, heavy baggage.

Only in recent years has my father begun to talk about his experiences during and after the war, and he had never spoken about them in public before. Without notes, and with a clarity that bespoke how sharply these events are etched in my father's memory, he recounted his tale.

After most of the Jewish population of his hometown of Czenstochowa, in western Poland, was deported to Treblinka (including his father and sister), my father, who had been active in the Jewish underground, was captured with forged papers that identified him as a South American citizen. For the last two years of the war, he was held in a POW camp in Germany. As soon as he was freed, he recalled at the conference, he was asked to help liberate a group of Jews who were still on a death march from Buchenwald. This group formed the nucleus of a DP camp that my father set up and ran in the years after the war.

Where did his strength come from in those years, I wondered? How did all these survivors manage to carry on? On a more self-centered note, I wondered what I could ever recount to my children that could compare to the heroism and daring displayed by my father and his peers during their youth? Obviously, this was a heroism they had not chosen, and would have all preferred to have done without. But how they rose to that challenge, how they almost literally lifted themselves from the dead, is the true mystery and awe of those years.

The *Sh'erit ha-Pletah*, or "surviving remnant," as the survivors chose to call themselves after the war, persevered so as to somehow bring redemption and meaning to those who were murdered. In so doing, they not only survived; they transformed the world. Elie Wiesel said at the conference that "for survivors, every day is an act of grace; every gesture, an offering." We, their children, can aspire to no less.

Passover, the Process

April 1999

It's probably safe to say that if you're reading this column right now, you're stuck at home for Passover.

I mean "stuck," of course, only in the most positive sense of the word. Every year at this time, in an act reminiscent of the original Exodus, thousands of Jews gather together their extended families, pack up all their worldly possessions, and head for the Promised Land. The Promised Land, in this case, usually means a hotel in the Poconos, but it extends as far as Florida, Arizona, and sometimes even the Promised Land itself.

The big difference, of course — and the key to the whole experience — is that in this Exodus, the Jews don't have to bring the matzah.

Now, don't get me wrong. Some of my best friends go to hotels for Pesach, and I have spent most of my life envious of them. This envy only intensified after I started making Pesach in my own home several years ago. The thought of not having to turn my house on its head and spend hours shopping for overpriced goods and cooking 14 different matzah meal-based recipes — talk about liberation from slavery!

Instead, I have to rely on a fresh perspective to make the arduous seem less so, and remind me of some of the actual pleasures of making Passover at home.

"It's here! Pesach is here!" shouted my son, as he awoke about two weeks before the holiday and discovered half the Passover dishes already unpacked in the kitchen. He heralded the coming of the holiday with the excitement otherwise reserved for the arrival of a beloved guest or a new toy. And suddenly, the task of converting my kitchen for Passover use seemed a little less awful.

I, too, remember taking special delight in helping my mother arrange the kitchen in its special Passover format, with all the dishes out on display and the freshly laundered doilies lining the counters. Passover was not just a holiday, it was a process. There was the process of cleaning my room, the process of taking out the Pesach dishes, the process of picking out the most potent stalk of *maror*.

And somehow, that process led to transformation. There was the magic that descends upon a household when important guests are expected, when everything is familiar and yet all dolled up and wonderfully different.

Now, as an adult, I know that magic to be a thin disguise for the nervous energy that builds up as the guests threaten to walk in the door imminently. But for my kids, the magic seems to have endured. As soon as Purim was over, they were jumping up and down in anticipation of Pesach.

My seven-year-old already knows the routine. He wanted to know which day we were getting our hair cut, which day we would be getting new shoes, which day we would go shopping for the shankbone and the bitter herbs. He wanted to know who was coming for the seders and where everyone was going to sit. He carefully helped me unpack our Passover dishes, and made sure we had brought with us all the seder paraphernalia he and his brother had made for Pesachs past.

We're celebrating Pesach in our new house for the first time this year, and the process of making Pesach here is a process of truly making this our home.

When you've finally unpacked the boxes that say "Passover dishes" on them, you know you're home. We all participated in trying to figure out how to organize the kitchen, deciding which counters and cabinets would hold our Pesach wares.

In fact, for almost a month now, my kids have been following me around the house, wanting to know what I'm up to and how it will pertain to Pesach. Why did we buy a caseload of grape juice? Why can't we eat pretzels in the den anymore? Why are we all getting new toothbrushes? Each question leads to a whole conversation about how different Pesach is from the rest of the year. It's like the Four Questions, only it's about 40 questions. By the time the holiday arrives, the kids will feel very much a part of it.

And, of course, that's the point no matter where you celebrate the holiday. Pesach is a big deal and involves preparation, of different kinds. The idea of "making" Pesach is the sense of making Pesach your own — making the seders run in a way that is meaningful to your family, making your home, or maybe even your hotel room, conform to the traditions you want to endure and the innovations you want to introduce each year.

When I sit down for that first seder, after all the weeks of preparation, I continue another tradition that I learned in my parents' home. I collapse in my chair, and loudly complain about how exhausted I am. Then I survey the family and friends gathered around the beautifully set table, and begin the seder song.

Chag Kasher V'Sameach.

A Soccer Kicks into the New Year

October 2000

So I've finally become a soccer mom. You do not join this elite demographic simply by attending a soccer game or two. Oh no. To attain this status, you must reach that point in modern American parenthood where the chief role you play in your children's lives is that of chauffeur. Or cruise director.

I spend many an evening coordinating carpools for various extracurricular activities, and many an afternoon driving an assorted number of children to those activities. And if, heaven forfend, there is a free afternoon in my child's week, I have to arrange a playdate or some other diversion to entertain him or her. Sundays? Fuhggedaboutit. My kids already start asking me on Friday what we're doing on Sunday, and if I respond that they have, among them, three birthday parties and two soccer games, one will inevitably ask, OK, and what are we doing after that?

Now, I realize it is I who have allowed this state of affairs to come to pass. I'm the one standing on line for two hours and forking over one hundred dollars each for the privilege of having to drive my sons to soccer practice twice a week.

And, fool that I am, I'm trying to be a soccer mom while holding down a day job, which is exactly what this demographic is not supposed to have to worry about. Score another one for burning that proverbial candle at both ends.

So how exactly did I arrive at this point? I'm not sure. I actually did start this parenthood thing determined not to overprogram my children. I held out till the age of three to send them to preschool. I don't allow them more than one athletic activity per season. And I don't send them to camp for two months; I deliberately schedule some down time each summer, when they can practice the age-old childhood art of doing nothing.

And yet I don't want to deprive them of opportunities to pursue various interests. I enrolled my oldest son in a karate class as a bit of a lark, hoping it might improve his coordination. Who knew that four years later he'd be a blue belt? My younger son devotes time every week just to practicing his batting swing. I, his devoted mother, should not sign him up for Little League?

And this is not to mention the societal and peer pressure — on my kids, and on me. Yes, they're the ones coming home from school telling me that everybody is joining whatever. But I also don't want to be the only parent saying no all the time. So my well-thought-out compromise is this: I just say no some of the time.

I have been musing on all this as the school year has gone into full swing. I am amazed at how full my life is right now. I mean this in the logistical sense of the term — I am busy basically all the time. Thankfully, this is all good busy, as I am fond of saying. But sometimes, even good busy doesn't leave a lot of room for anything but keeping your head above water.

This is why God created Rosh HaShanah and Yom Kippur and the whole High Holy Days season. And He placed these Days of Awe right now, when the summer doldrums give way to the post-Labor Day work crunch, when the school year gets under way, when the soccer season is at its height. Because in His wisdom He knew, as we all do, that there's more to life than all this.

Now is the time to pause and take stock, and make sure that all this busy-ness does not leave us without time to cultivate less hectic pursuits — like spending time with our families, reading some good books, learning some Torah, and giving back to our communities. We don't do this only for ourselves; our children are watching to see how we determine our priorities.

It is a time to sort through all the stuff that makes up our daily lives and make sure that we are spending our lives the way we really want to, the way we may have once dreamed of doing. It is a time to reach once again for those dreams, in case we have lost our way.

And it is a time, most of all, to count our blessings, hold our loved ones near and pray for good health, peace and prosperity for all of *Klal Yisrael*.

L'shanah Tova Tikatayvu V'Techataymu. Happy New Year.

Life in the Present Tense

March 2002

Purim just passed and that must mean Passover is right around the corner...

This is how I might have begun a column a year ago. More to the point, this is how my thinking would have gone a year ago, or at any time in my life until now. One milestone, or holiday, or event down; on to planning the next. I would do what I needed to do each day, but always with one eye on the next project, the next undertaking, even if it was only planning who to have over for Shabbat lunch.

Time seemed to me like an unbroken continuum. Life stretched before me open-ended, with various red-letter days along the way that I could look forward to, plan and savor in anticipation. If I had a problem with time, it was that, between my job, my family, and my community, there was never enough of it each day. But I never questioned that there was an order to life, one thing following another, always moving inexorably forward. Everything I did today was an investment in reaching a goal for the future.

No more. I am now on cancer time. Cancer time puts an end to this kind of thinking. The future is, at best, uncertain; at worst, bleak. I can no longer peer down the road and look forward to the bar mitzvahs, the graduations, the career highlights, the new kitchen. The future now stretches about as far as next week, and even that is hard to plan.

Cancer time forces you solidly into the present, and to some extent, into the past. Today is really the only day you can count on. People keep urging me to take things "one day at a time" with this disease. Sometimes, in fact, it feels more like one hour at a time, 15 minutes at a time. It's almost like reverting to a child-like state, where there's no such thing as delayed gratification and no thought given to tomorrow. On the other hand, I have infinite patience; where am I rushing off to these days?

Not surprisingly, it is with my children that I feel this live-in-the-moment sensation most acutely. Everything I do with them is infused with meaning. The most important thing I did last week, for example, was to go bowling with my kids. First of all, I showed up, which for me these days is half the battle. And though I couldn't even bowl, I was really and truly there. No work deadlines loomed over me, no phone calls needed to be returned; nothing else really mattered that afternoon other than watching the pins go down and whooping it up with my kids.

A friend of mine who lives in Jerusalem told me that I am now starting to think and act like an Israeli. Americans, he says, are always planning. We plan our bar mitzvahs two years in advance, we plan summer camp the previous fall, we spend months and sometimes years planning additions to our houses. In Israel, he says, you have no idea if you'll get blown up on a bus tomorrow or if your teenager will make it home from the mall. So you take life as it comes, one morning, one afternoon, one evening at a time.

Every morning I can send my kids off to school, do a few things around the house, and feel well, is a good morning. Every afternoon that I can greet my children, eat dinner, and do homework, is a good afternoon. Every bedtime story that I can read, every goodnight kiss delivered and received, is a good ending to the evening. There are many, many bad days with this disease; every good day is exactly that: a good day, a victory of sorts.

String a bunch of good days together, and you actually end up moving into the future, without actually planning it. You also create a past and a storehouse of memories for yourself and your children. I am starting to share some of my personal memories with my children so that they are carried forward. And I am aware that in imbuing the present with such meaning, I am hoping to create good memories for my children to draw upon down the road.

In a way, of course, this is what we do as a people. Whether I am planning for it or not, Pesach will surely come later this month. More than most holidays, Pesach reminds us that the past is very much a part of the present and is also the cornerstone for our future. Even as we enjoy the seder very much in the present, gathered around with our families, we retell the story of the Exodus every year as if we ourselves are experiencing it.

At the same time, we re-enact our own families' seder traditions, bequeathing our personal memories to our children.

In a way, we merge different aspects of time at the seder. And though my illness has changed my perspective on what I can and cannot plan on, it has reaffirmed my faith in the longer term. For there, sitting at my seder table, will be three generations of my family, celebrating together our family's and our people's cherished traditions. And therein already lies my future.

I would like to thank all the many well-wishers who responded so kindly to my last column. May we be privileged to share in *b'sorot tovot*, good tidings, for all our people. And let me wish you all a *chag kasher v'sameach*.

Israel at 54: an Existential Threat

April 2002

Seven blown up on a bus near Afula. Five boys killed at their yeshiva in Atzmona. A teenager gunned down on a street in Kfar Saba. An entire family wiped out leaving shul on a Saturday night. A couple and their unborn child killed after getting an ultrasound in downtown beloved, beleaguered Jerusalem.

The numbers are numbing, the incidents begin to blur. It's hard to keep track of how many died in what town, in which venue. Each time you hear of an attack, you rush to contact your closest friends or relatives. Once you ascertain that they are fine, you scan the paper to see if the names ring a bell anyway. Then, you wring your hands, maybe wipe away a tear, and then go back to work, or back to the breakfast you were eating, or back to the screaming kids riding behind you in the minivan.

It's not that we don't care. We do. We care very much. Those of us with close and deep ties to Israel and its residents are in agony over the recent events there. We speak to our family and friends; we know how harrowing life is for them now, how fearful they are to go out at night or let their children go out with their friends. Sending their kids off to school in the morning, an activity most of us regard as a godsend, is a terrifying act for many of them. Will they return in the afternoon?

My eight-year-old niece, who lives in Jerusalem, is practicing drills she learned in school on what to do if she hears an explosion or gunfire. My friend in Raanana has revoked her newly independent 12-year-old daughter's right to take the bus by herself to school; it's the same line that goes through Kfar

Saba and has been attacked once too often. Friends in Beit Shemesh and Chashmonaim say they do not travel to Jerusalem, or much of anywhere else, anymore. They have become virtual prisoners in cocoons of their own making, circumscribed areas that they have somehow deemed relatively safe.

These concessions may seem relatively minor. I am fortunate that no one I know personally has been directly involved in any of the attacks. But the ripple effect is enormous. As hard as it may be to keep track of how many have died in each incident, most of us don't even bother taking note of the number injured, or the number of eyewitnesses who will forever be traumatized, or the number of people attending way too many funerals, or the number of family members whose lives are torn asunder.

For every person killed, a family is left to grieve. For every person wounded, family and friends are left to care for them. Their injuries may be serious enough that they require long hospital stays or a long recuperation at home. The financial costs might be staggering, especially if a breadwinner is disabled, or if a home needs to be retrofitted to accommodate a wheelchair. Just from the Atzmona attack alone, the injured included a young man who is now paralyzed from the waist down, another who had his foot amputated, and yet another who suffered serious internal injuries.

And then there is the sheer, constant, omnipresent fear and anxiety. Every day, without letup. Think back to the terror that struck us on September 11 and the anxiety we all felt in the days and weeks that followed. Remember when we were afraid to fly or even drive through a tunnel? Remember when we feared going to popular or crowded attractions, like a ballgame or a parade? Remember being afraid to open your mail lest some anthrax fall out?

These fears have now faded for most of us; in fact, they seem almost quaint in recollection.

In Israel, however, those fears are real and founded and still very much present. Perhaps, having recently been diagnosed with cancer, I have a new appreciation for those living in the shadow of death. It hangs like a cloud over everything you do and it makes the business of living all that more urgent and precious. It also puts an oppressive strain on family and friends.

It is in this spirit that I applaud all those trying to help the secondary and tertiary victims of terror in Israel, those like the Israel Emergency Solidarity Fund who are trying to raise funds for families of the victims. And Kol Haneshama, a group of Yeshiva University students publishing mini-profiles of those who were killed to help personalize each victim. Read these profiles. They are instructive on the enormity of each life lost and all those lives they have changed forever.

Yom Ha'atzmaut, Israel Independence Day, is upon us. We who were born after the establishment of the State of Israel have taken its existence — however difficult — for granted all our lives. For too long we have let our brothers and sisters in Israel alone stake out our independence as a people.

But make no mistake. If the events in Israel continue as they are, the very existence of this grand post-Holocaust renewal of the Jewish people will be on the line.

If I may quote from Ginette Lando, who lost her 16-year-old daughter to a bomb in a Ginot Shomron pizzeria, and whose words are published on the Israel Emergency Solidarity Fund's Web site: "This war, and it is just that, a war against us as a people, us as Jews, and us as a nation, may go on forever, but we must never give up and must never run away." On this Yom Ha'atzmaut, let us take nothing for granted.

The Hardest Year

September 2002

It's been one tough year.

It began, of course, with September 11, which fell last year just a few days before Rosh HaShanah. None of us will soon forget the sheer horror of that day, and the fear and anxiety that pervaded the following weeks. Then the intifada in Israel, which had started the previous year around Rosh HaShanah as well, picked up and intensified. Somehow, perhaps because of September 11 or perhaps just because of the frequency and numbers involved, each attack in Israel seemed to hit home more powerfully than the one before. We took it personally this year, in a way that many of us never did before.

And then, in my own little world, I was diagnosed with cancer — a disease with which I am still struggling — and the bottom just fell out from under me.

As Rosh HaShanah approaches again, I must admit that my faith in a benevolent God has been sorely tested. I have always believed in God. Why, I couldn't tell you; like most believers, I suppose, I cannot give a rational explanation for my faith. But I do know that this faith has guided me and sustained me my whole life. At the same time, I have always known that evil exists and that seemingly random tragedies, from car accidents to fatal diseases, happen all the time. I need look no further than the Holocaust to question the very beliefs upon which I have built my religious observance, and indeed, my whole way of life.

Nothing like cancer to make me realize how succoured I had been in my beliefs until now. It's not that hard to believe in a God that granted most of my wishes. I had a loving, wonderful family, great friends, and a satisfying career. What was not to like? Tragedy was something that happened to other people. Certainly I felt for those who suffered, and I traveled last year to Poland in part to understand more deeply what had been lost to the Jewish people and to my own family in the Holocaust. My Jewish observance depended in part on the belief that by continuing in the faith of my ancestors, I could somehow bring redemption to those who had suffered.

But now it is I who suffer, and my former notions of redemption and meaning seem so glib — as they must have seemed to all the people I tried them on in the past. I have a new sense of profound respect for those who have suffered. In fact, though I have asked God repeatedly: "Why me?" I understand that the real question is: "Why not me?" This was the response that came from a friend who had lost her father at a young age and whose husband was also fighting cancer. Instead of the question that came so naturally to me — What did I do to deserve such a fate? — her approach, so humbling and so refined, was: Am I so special that I should avoid such a fate? Tragedy strikes so many people, many more meritorious than I, so why not me?

I need only look to Israel to understand what she meant. So many innocents there have died, including Jews who have devoted themselves much more fully than I have to the service of God and His land. And since getting sick, so many people that I thought led perfectly ordinary lives have come forward and shared with me their own difficult experiences. This brings me back to the more general question, Why should anybody have to suffer? Great philosophers and theologians have tackled this most profound of questions; I do not presume to have anywhere near the answer.

But I have spent the better part of these past few months asking the question of many wise people. A revered teacher of mine recently suggested at least an approach. We have no control over what fate or God hands us. This has been made crystal clear to all of us this past year. But we can, to some extent, shape our response to what comes our way. If I understand correctly, Maimonides wrote that when faced with hardships, one should do *teshuvah*, repentance. This is not because the travails are necessarily a punishment for any specific sin; rather, they can serve as a stimulant to re-examine your life and see if there's anything you might be able to do differently. It's a chance, possibly, to move to another level — in relationships with family and friends, in showing kindness to those in even greater need, and even in faith in God. Stripped of many of the mundane concerns that once seemed to me all-consuming, I have almost been forced into this re-examination of what's important and where I could do better.

As I enter these days of awe, I am of course praying for a *refuah sheleimah* — a complete recovery, for myself and for many others who have taken ill. And I am praying for peace in Israel and here in the United States and an end to all the bloodshed. But I am also praying to God — this very God who perplexes me so — to help me rise to the challenges with which I've been presented, and indeed the challenges facing all of us these days. We are, in individual and communal ways, being asked to step up to the new realities of our time. Ultimately, these may prove to be the defining moments of our lives.

May God give us strength. And whatever strength we cannot find in our search for Him, let us find in one another.

L'Shanah Tova Tikatayvu V'Teychataymu. May it be a better year.

Mothers and Feminism

December 2002

I went last month to the Orthodoxy and Feminism Conference knowing the hot topics of the day would revolve around issues such as dress, modesty, and women getting called to the Torah in Orthodox congregations. But I came away from the event with something unexpected: a renewed appreciation for the power of a mother's love.

On the first night of the conference, Isaiah Sheffer read aloud "Sarah's Story," an extraordinary short story by a relatively unknown writer named Galina Vromen. Told from the perspective of our matriarch Sarah, it is the story of a mother's reaction upon being told by her husband that he wants to sacrifice their son to God. "Are you mad?" she asks Abraham.

Now, I've been taught the story of the sacrifice of Isaac every which way — but never have I given much thought to Sarah's role in the drama. And suddenly, it was so obvious: what other reaction could a mother have? She's waited 90 years to bear a child, she finally gets the joy of raising a son, and now she's just going to let him be taken away to be slaughtered? Even if it was so ordained by God?

In Vromen's story, God and Abraham combined are no match for a mother propelled by grief. The aged matriarch secretly follows Abraham and Isaac to Mount Moriah; there, she hires a shepherd to hide behind a bush and impersonate God. It is this shepherd who commands Abraham to stop the knife from falling on Isaac's neck, and it is the hidden Sarah who sends the ram into Abraham's sight so that he will sacrifice it instead of his son. Later, when Abraham recounts the story and tells how God commanded him to stop, Sarah smiles quietly to herself.

I don't know if this Sarah was a feminist, but she certainly acted on her instincts as a mother. Blu Greenberg, founding president of the Jewish Orthodox Feminist Alliance, is a self-described feminist; has been for at least 30 years. But she too is a mother, a mother who recently lost one of her sons, J.J. Despite her grief — or perhaps because of it — there she stood at the conference before a thousand men and women, bravely honoring her son's memory, giving his life meaning as part of a greater whole.

"I feel that J.J.'s life embodied what this conference is all about," she said. "Because... this conference is more than an articulation of new roles and responsibilities [for women]. It's really about the basic dignity of every human being created in the image of God. And the reason I connect this to J.J. is that that's how he lived his life. He understood this about women. He treated men and women as equals and respected their dignity."

Talk about dignity. It practically radiated from Ms. Greenberg as she spoke. And it was not just the love and pride she took in her son that informed her dignity; it was the sense that her son and his cherished memory had in turn given her the strength to speak to these thousand strangers and connect his life to theirs.

I know from my own personal battle with cancer that it is my children who give me the strength to endure. They are the ones who keep me going, who make it worthwhile to get out of bed each morning and somehow cope with the difficulties of the disease. They are the ones who help me make some sense out of my present and give me faith in a future. Whatever love we give our children we get back from them tenfold in strength and in hope.

As I looked around the room at the JOFA conference, I saw scattered in the crowd dozens of young mothers holding infants, and many older mothers sitting with teenage or adult daughters. These mothers come to these conferences because they want their daughters' and sons' lives to be steeped in their Jewish heritage, but also engaged in a Jewish future. They are willing to risk community censure because they believe that what they are doing will make their children's lives richer, fuller and perhaps even more dignified.

Knowing how far they've come and what obstacles still remain, these women are staking their faith firmly in the future. Whatever advances they make today will benefit them, but, more importantly, will lay the groundwork for their children. In my opinion — and this may not be widely shared — feminism, at least as it is manifested at events like JOFA's, is yet another facet of maternal love, particularly of a Jewish mother's love. At its heart, it is an effort by mothers willing to take risks in order to make life better for their children. And this vision for their children gives these mothers the strength they need to carry on.

Saddam and Passover

April 2003

So I kind of had things figured out. Bush was going to strike Iraq on Purim and I had this whole "Iraq equals Persia/Hussein equals Haman" cosmic connection going.

Actually, it was my nine-year-old who tipped me off to the connection. Trying to follow world events while keeping up with your schoolwork is not easy. In conversation, he was constantly referring to Hussein as Haman, to the Arabs as Germans, and to Amalek as the Palestinians. After awhile, instead of correcting him, I began to realize that they really are all one big mishmash of hatred and violence that has lasted for centuries.

Still, the parallels for this latest war seemed so compelling (Condoleeza Rice as Queen Esther?) and so "*bashert*," or fated. By Passover, I figured — the holiday of freedom — the Iraqis would be set free and we would see a new era dawn in the Middle East, including, naturally, peace for Israel.

Sounds pretty good, huh? I shudder to contemplate the possibility that President Bush actually sees the conflict in these types of biblical, apocalyptic, and ultimately simplistic terms. The reality, of course, is much more complicated, although perhaps no less absurd. As the widely circulated e-mail joke has it: You know the world is going crazy when the best rapper is a white guy; the best golfer is a black guy; the Swiss hold the Americas Cup; France is accusing the U.S. of arrogance; and Germany doesn't want to go to war.

In short, we live in a world gone mad. Or perhaps we have just gone back to business as usual. Let's face it: The last 50 or 60 years, when most of us were growing up and building our lives, were an aberration in world and Jewish history. We just didn't realize what a blip those years turned out to be. For centuries, the world, and Jews in particular, were more often than not in a state of war and/or persecution and deprivation. But after World War II, the Western world entered a period of widespread economic well being and international stability. And Jews, in possession of our own country for the first time in 2,000 years, enjoyed an era of prosperity and freedom from persecution unparalleled in our history.

I got to think of this as normal, or at least, a new normal. And why shouldn't I? It was the only reality I knew. I figured we, as a people and as a part of the larger world, had suffered enough. We had all learned our lessons in World War II and that was the end of that. Good had triumphed over evil at long last. And while I did not believe we lived in exactly messianic times, I could not imagine a return to the chaos and suffering of previous generations.

Now, the Holocaust this isn't. And most of us, particularly in the United States, are still living our lives much the way we were, say, before September 11. But a new awareness has come over us. We are more aware of our vulnerability, more aware of the capriciousness of life, more aware of the existence of evil in this world. We are also more aware of how quickly our lives can change because of events taking place seemingly far away. One Scud missile thrown in Israel's direction, one more anti-Semitic incident in France, one more terrorist incident on these shores — and who knows?

What we do with this new awareness is for each of us to decide. Me, I've got cancer. I don't need the outside world to remind me how short our time is on Earth and how much we have to squeeze out of every minute. But there are moments, or occasions, that highlight this feeling even more so than usual.

Passover is one such occasion. Whatever I may feel about the dubious notion of "liberating" the Iraqi people, Passover is indeed the festival of freedom. And it is something to relish the unprecedented freedom we have in this era in this country and Israel. Passover is also the holiday of redemption. Now that we are somewhat better acquainted with hardship, we can more deeply appreciate the yearnings of untold generations of Jews who longed for redemption and the promise of a better world.

And finally, at least as it is practiced today, Passover is also the holiday of family. More so than the High Holy Days, when we spend most of the time in synagogue, often lost in our own thoughts, Pesach is the holiday of home and hearth. Most of us try to get together with parents, siblings, cousins, friends; we tend to make our seders large and boisterous — the more kids, the more comments, the better. It is an ingathering of our loved ones, much as we hope for an ingathering of all the exiled in the days to come.

This year, perhaps more than most, we will gather everyone very close, and hold them very tight. Who knows but that this is the true beginning of redemption.

My Father's Words

May 2003

My father has run out of words. He has been ill for some time, but in the last few weeks he has retreated into a world of his own. He eats, he drinks, he smiles, he nods. But, with some rare exceptions, he is no longer using words. He no longer seems to hear what others are saying (although I sometimes suspect he does), and he no longer responds to people in words. His eyes seem focused elsewhere. At times, he seems to be grasping for a lost expression, for a forgotten word. But for the most part, he has lapsed into silence.

I became a writer in no small measure because my father had been one. During his aborted young adulthood in pre-war Poland, he worked for a Yiddish newspaper in his hometown and resumed writing in a DP camp publication after the war. Upon arrival in the United States, however, like so many immigrants and refugees, he had to put aside his more creative aspirations and earn a living. He found a job in the garment industry, and stayed there until he retired more than 40 years later.

He never disguised the fact that he hated the business world. It wore him down. Writing remained his passion. He wrote periodically for a Yiddish newspaper in New York over the years. After he retired, the gig turned into a regular weekly column and became a nearly full-time occupation for him. He used his column to opine about everything from Israeli politics to former President Clinton's infidelities.

But mostly, he used the column to bear witness. Most of his columns ended up, one way or the other, back in Poland. Either they recounted an experience of his during the war, or marked the anniversary of a significant event, or used a modern-day example to show how the Holocaust still reverberated today. My father felt strongly that the world, and Jews in particular, had not learned adequately the lessons of the Shoah, or the *Churban*, as he called it. We were all too ready to forgive and forget, to move on — something he felt was a disgrace to the martyrs and a move that we made at our own peril.

Words, words, words; testimony, documents, papers — this is what my father believed in as the only way to influence opinion and preserve memory.

And now silence. I know I am not alone in watching an aging parent decline. It is nothing short of heartbreaking. You keep searching, in the gaze of their eyes, in the lines on their face, in the movement of their hands, for the parent you once knew. What you see before you is the shell. And so you too find yourself retreating into memory. At the seder last month, I closed my eyes and saw my father at the head of the table, leading the ritual, as he always had. As the war in Iraq raged, I heard in my head the arguments he and I would have had over the justifications for this fight and its long-term implications.

And certainly, on Yom Hashoah, which we just commemorated this week, I thought of how often he'd remarked in recent years about how his generation was dying off, and who would be left to remember? I would assure him that my generation would continue the legacy, and that we were in turn passing this mandate on to our children. I am not sure he was convinced.

With each passing survivor, he would lament, there is one less person to tell about the life we led before the destruction; one less person to give testimony; one less person who had to live with the nightmare day in, day out; one less person who could keep alive the memory of someone who perished.

One less person who would have the words to shout out to the world: We are here. We survived.

And yet, of course, they have left words for us. Some survivors, no doubt, could never bring themselves to speak of their experiences. But others, like my father, spent a lifetime recording their stories. Some became world-famous writers and de facto spokesmen for their generation; others simply told their stories to their children, or perhaps donated their words to a museum or videotape project.

But the writing, the retelling, cannot stop with them. True, only the survivors could actually bear witness. But our generation, particularly the children of survivors, must continue to remind the world. We must bear witness to the fact that there were witnesses. We must tell and retell our parents' stories, much as we tell and retell the story of our Exodus from Egypt each year on Passover. We must give voice to those who no longer have a voice. Yes, the voice is one step removed, but we must ensure that the stories, as told by our children, will one day be two steps removed, and then three steps, and so on.

It's not just that we owe it to our parents. We owe it to ourselves, to our people, to our children. From those who came to this country with nothing, it is our most precious inheritance. It is our legacy. It is our tribute.

A Tale of Two Cities

September 2003

I live in a thriving Jewish community. I look about me and see new houses going up all the time, kids tumbling out of every one of them. I hear the conversations in the kosher restaurants or at the local grocery about choices of schools, career options, investments in stocks or real estate. I go online to our very own listserve, TeaneckShuls, and read the dozens of postings each day — people trading in everything from contractors to carpools, from babysitters to Yankee tickets.

This was the town I moved to nearly 10 years ago. I knew it would be a great place to raise my kids and live a Modern Orthodox lifestyle. It would also be a community where I could find like-minded peers — ambitious, bright women and men combining successful careers with family life and communal and intellectual pursuits.

But then, nearly two years ago, I was diagnosed with cancer. And a whole new town opened up to me. This one lies just beneath the surface of the other, more familiar one. I entered into this alternative universe unwillingly, but now that I am firmly entrenched in it, I continue to marvel at how active and challenging and engaging it can be.

Behind the facades of many a home unfortunately lie families in distress. There is illness, sometimes chronic, sometimes acute; there is unemployment or economic hardship; there are difficult marriages, unhappy adults, straying children. None of this is unique to my community, of course. In fact, these are the cliches of suburban life: no one could possibly live up to the pristine standards that the beautiful homes and manicured lawns would seem to suggest.

But what leaves me astounded is the myriad of individuals and groups that spring up, on their own initiative, to serve and aid those less fortunate than themselves. Now that my eyes have been opened to this underworld community, I see signs of it everywhere.

There's Project Ezrah, a grassroots organization that came into being when the economy went south, to help those in our community in need of financial assistance. There's the group of women who meet every Tuesday morning to recite Psalms for Jews around the world who are ill or are victims of terrorist attacks. There's the friend who attended clown school for six weeks in Philadelphia so that she can be well-trained when visiting the sick in local hospitals. And there's the group of amazing friends who banded together to help me on my new macrobiotic diet, forcing me to eat well, almost despite myself.

Mind you, these are not angels swooping down to repair the world. These are the very same people who take care of their families, pursue their careers, and carpool to soccer. They work quietly, often anonymously, on these acts of *chesed*, or kindness, and they get the job done. Needless to say, none of them ask for any money or any publicity or even any thanks in return. What "reward" they receive — if you could call it that — only they know in their hearts.

I am the first to admit that I used to be oblivious to this world of doing good. I'm not sure I even knew it existed. Of course, I gave my charitable donations to what I considered worthy causes, and I tried to help people out when I could. But my focus was inward: on my career, my family, my own circle of friends. I did a good deed when the opportunity presented itself. What I am learning, by contrast, is how people create opportunities to do a good deed. They don't wait for one to come knocking on their door.

The effect can be contagious, even in the smallest of gestures. The joke about TeaneckShuls is that people are always looking for a lift to somewhere. "Is anybody driving to Brooklyn on Friday?" "Can anybody take a package to Israel for me?" "Can someone drive my grandmother here from Monsey?" My initial, cynical reaction to these postings was: get your own car! But lately, I've been noticing a new trend online. People are now posting messages when they are driving somewhere and have space in their car. "Does anyone need a lift to Newark Airport? I'm going on Sunday and have room for two..." *Mitzvah goreret mitzvah* — one positive act leads to another, goes the Hebrew expression.

We are approaching the High Holy Day season. This has always been a period of introspection. In the past few years, between the breakout of the intifada in Israel and the attacks of September 11 — both of which occurred at around this time — the Days of Awe have also served as a kind of wake-up call. Clearly, there is much to be done on the world stage and too much, too much that needs to be remedied in Israel. But charity, as they say, begins at home. Look around you and listen closely. You too may find a way to help someone in need, be it by giving them a lift to midtown, or simply by giving them a reason to smile.

There's another Hebrew expression, the full meaning of which I have only learned these past couple of years. It's really more like a blessing, something you will say to another person after they have already done something wonderful. "*Tizku l'mitzvot*" — may you be worthy to perform additional positive commandments. It can truly be a "*z'chut*," a privilege, to perform an act of kindness for another. If nothing else, it means you are in a position to do so. I can think of no better wish for us all for this coming New Year.

L'shanah tova Tikatayvu V'Techataymu. Tizku l'mitzvot.

The View from Here

For I Have Been to the Mountain Top

February 1997

Lately, my son has been lobbying to go to Israel. At first I couldn't figure out what in recent months could have prompted this particular campaign.

Was the Jewish day school he started attending less than half a year ago already having an effect, imbuing in him the early stirrings of Zionist longing? Or, perhaps on a more familial level, since my husband's brother and his family live in Israel, did my son miss his aunt, uncle, and cousins, whom he hears about often but sees so rarely?

No, none of the above. It turns out my son's efforts were motivated by lofty thoughts only in the most literal sense of the word. The bottom line is that my five-year-old is currently infatuated with airplanes, and the only place he can think of flying to is Israel.

In fact, the only place anybody in our family ever talks about flying to is Israel. In the past year alone, my son has seen his grandmother, grandfather, and father each take trips to Israel. Little wonder then that he figures the only way he's ever going to get on a plane is to go to Israel.

Perhaps you are thinking, gee, this kid should get out more. Well, perhaps. But in a world of limited time and limited resources, my son picked up the message: In our family, if you get on a plane, chances are you're going to end up in Israel. At the grand old age of five, my son has already been there twice.

This is not a simple matter. It's not like we just enjoy vacationing in a country wracked by terrorist attacks, religious strife, and economic hardship. And in the course of my nine trips there and my husband's 14 (including each of us spending a year studying there), there aren't many tourist spots that we haven't hit.

Our pilgrimages to Israel obviously run deeper. In part, they are an attempt to maintain a closeness with relatives and friends who live there, most particularly my brother-in-law and his young family. And on another level still, they are an attempt to maintain a closeness with a dream; a dream, admittedly, that has lost much of its passion over the years.

The fact that I do not live in Israel still galls me. I am by no means a perfect Jew, and there are many *mitzvot* that I cannot or do not live up to. But making *aliyah* remains the one facet of my Judaism in which I still ardently believe but do not in the least bit practice. And I have no one to blame for this failure.

As a young adult, I was determined to move to Israel. Living in Israel was a fundamental tenet of my belief, as integral to my religion, I felt, as observing Shabbat or keeping kosher, and as integral to my political and nationalistic ideals as the vitality of the Jewish people itself. It was visceral. I knew this was not a view held by all, and I can't fully explain it. But I believed, with a conviction that I lacked about other ideas, that the only place for a Jew was in Israel.

But first, I just needed to get a good education in America. Then I just wanted to start my career here. Then I figured I'd have more luck finding a husband here. Then we needed to make some money. Then our parents began aging. Then we had children. Then we bought a house.

It's not that it is technically too late. But that old truism is coming to pass — the more roots you put down here, the harder it is to pick yourself up and go. And by the same token, the more commitments you make here, the more committed you become to staying. You get involved in a community, a synagogue, a school, organizations — pretty soon you realize that life as an American Jew can be filled with great meaning as well.

And so now, here I am, living in a community filled with lapsed Zionists. And I am repeating the cycle. I am raising my children to believe in the centrality of Israel, sending them to the same kind of day school that imbued in me the Zionist dream, and waiting for the day when they come home from school and ask me why I never moved to Israel. It's the same question I asked of my parents; like their answer, mine will only partly satisfy my children.

This dilemma is similar to one faced by all parents whenever they raise their children to believe in ideals that they themselves cannot always live up to. It is like teaching the importance of charity, and then walking past the homeless man on the street. Or, on a more mundane level, telling the kids to shut off the TV, and then collapsing in front of that same television after they've gone to bed.

We have learned to live with these contradictions. We understand some of the nuances that our children cannot, and we have rationalized the rest away. We can only hope our children will do us one better. That is why we bother to teach the ideal, that is why we repeat the cycle. If we can't always be the perfect role models, at least we can pass along our hopes and aspirations.

Every time our family visits Israel, I feel we are letting our children take hold of our dream.

My Own Personal Boycott

February 1999

Is it just me, or has anyone noticed a creeping German takeover of corporate America?

Actually, *The Wall Street Journal* recently ran a front page story comparing the outcry that arose in the 1980s when Japanese companies started taking over American corporate icons, with the complete apathy that has marked Americans' reaction to German acquisitions in the past couple of years.

Some recent examples: Daimler-Benz, maker of Mercedes, bought Chrysler last year, making it the largest car manufacturer in the world; Bertelsmann A.G. acquired Random House, making it one of the largest publishing conglomerates in the world; and took over Bankers Trust, solidifying the German bank's pre-eminence.

So what? We live in a global economy. Nationalism is dead. The only thing that really matters to these companies is money, and as long as they keep turning a profit, who cares whether the conglomerate is "German" or "American," or any other nationality, for that matter?

I do — as politically incorrect as that may sound. First off, I don't buy the argument that nationalism is dead, and that its darker side cannot rise again. Nationalism seems alive and well in what's left of the former Yugoslavia, for example. But I am not knowledgeable enough to argue this case effectively.

What I do know is much more personal. After a lifetime of conscientiously never buying a German product, the banal Chrysler minivan sitting in my driveway has suddenly been transformed into a Mercedes. And this galls me. I've already told my husband that our next minivan (God help us!) will not be a Dodge Caravan.

I may be the last of a dying breed. Several months ago, *The New York Times Magazine* ran a piece by a man who professed never to have bought a German-made product — until then. He just couldn't resist the allure of the new Volkswagen Beetle. Finally, he decided, the war was over.

I have never felt I had the right to declare an end to this particular war. From early childhood, I was brought up to believe that we should never forget what the Germans did to our people, to our family. This belief pervaded our very being, and no gesture in memoriam was considered too small.

Buying a German product was as anathema to my family as eating *treif*. Doing so would be an acknowledgement that the world was back to normal, all was forgiven, Germany was just another country. In our family, at least, that would never be true.

I am not naive enough to believe that by my not buying a Peter Kaiser shoe or a Dodge Caravan, the German economy will topple and fall. My personal "boycott," I know, is meaningless on an economic level.

But since when does Jewish ritual or Jewish memory or Jewish tradition depend on its effect on the outside world? I boycott German products not to make an impact on Germany, but to make an impact on myself.

You can always tell an observant Jew in a supermarket: they are the ones turning food items upside down to hunt for a telltale sign that the products are kosher. This is akin to what I do when I check for the "Made in Germany" mark.

It takes an extra minute, but it is an extra minute to remind myself that I am different, I am apart; in this age of consumerism, I can't buy everything.

At our greatest simchas, we recite the verse from Psalms that we will never forget thee, O Jerusalem, we will always set the destruction of Jerusalem above our highest joy. Do we care that Jerusalem in our day seems already to have been rebuilt? We recite the verse to remind ourselves that appearances may be deceiving. Indeed, all is not well. We have not yet been made whole.

So too, I think, with the destruction of European Jewry. It has been more than 50 years since the Holocaust, and we have indeed rebuilt ourselves in Israel and America. But the loss we have suffered is immeasurable, and the mourning is not over. My father and his generation of survivors will always have their acute memories; I need other devices, some seemingly trivial, to keep the memory burning.

Sometimes, mourning is in the details.

Reflections at a Ball Game

May 1999

We are deep in the heart of Little League season, and like millions of parents across the land, there I stood on Sunday afternoon engaged in what can only be described as the quintessential American pastime: cheering for my son's team.

The scene was idyllic: my son at bat, my husband and older son coaching from the sidelines, my little daughter playing on the swings nearby. Around me were dozens of kids and parents involved in similar activities. It looked for all the world like a typical, carefree suburban setting.

But here in my Modern Orthodox shtetl, the sounds of the game were different. "Yaakov, hold the bat higher!" "Ari, keep your eye on the ball!" "Run home, Sarah, run home!"

And so, I thought, the transformation was complete. The great-grandchildren of the original shtetls in Europe, carrying the names of their murdered forebears, were running the bases in America. And these children, for the most part, were blissfully unaware of all that came before them.

Now, I'll admit: most parents watching their kids' Little League games don't start thinking about the Holocaust. That might just be me. I can't seem to get over the fact that this is how I spend my Sunday afternoons: in perfect normalcy, raising my children in such a mundane fashion. I marvel sometimes not only at how far my children have traveled from their grandparents' shattered lives, but how distant they are even from my own youth.

I am the daughter of the saddest generation in Jewish history, and the mother, arguably, of the happiest. Never before have Jews been so secure, so prosperous, so free — in the Diaspora and in Israel. And this, only two generations after the most devastating event in our history.

My generation, the one born in the immediate wake of the Shoah, is the one in between. And in between is how I often feel. While of course I did not endure any of the horrors of the Holocaust, I grew up directly in its shadow. And in my home, at least, it cast a very long shadow. I grew up with all the trappings of a middle class, observant lifestyle, but there was a sadness that pervaded my home, a despair that nothing could shake.

I have no recollection of specifically being told about the Holocaust; just a constant sense that things were not quite right, that this world was a darker and more forbidding place than I could ever know. I saw it in the way my father sat up late at night, the house dark except for one lone light over his chair, and him just holding his head in his hand. I heard it in the sounds of my mother crying in her sleep. I felt it when I tried to discuss why I had no grandparents and was met with half-answers.

Way before I understood anything about the Holocaust, I knew that I bore a tremendous responsibility — a responsibility to right a terrible wrong, and somehow make up to my parents what they had lost; and a responsibility to carry on, and to preserve my heritage.

This was my *yerusha*, my inheritance, and as terrible as it is, it is now my responsibility to pass it on to my children. This is no easy task. My husband and I have started to talk to our oldest, who is seven, about the Holocaust, and he knows that his grandparents — on both sides — went through a bad thing. But the tragedy is not palpable in our home; it can't be, it shouldn't be.

I am thrilled that I am able, so far, to give my children a childhood largely free of worry and sadness. It is a blessing I try never to take for granted.

But although this may sound antithetical to the very essence of parenting, I must somehow introduce to them the notion of loss. I must teach them about all that we have lost, as a family and as a people, and not just because I want them to appreciate what they have. It is because this is part of who they are and where they come from. I believe that their generation, like mine, cannot build a future without a firm foundation in its past. It was hard for my parents to talk about their experiences; it is my obligation to never stop talking.

As part of the generation in between, I am a conduit. I do not wish to pass on to my children the ghosts that hovered over my childhood, but I also do not wish for them to be ignorant of their history. To bequeath my *yerusha*, I may have to bring some darkness into my children's lives. But they, in turn, will show my parents the light.

Land of Macs and Honey

October 1999

If it's Tuesday, it must be Burger King... and the Kotel.

That about sums up my family's recent vacation in Israel. I use the word "vacation" loosely, since, as any parent will attest — a vacation is what you need when you get back from traveling with your children.

There is nothing quite like hauling your children 6,000 miles to soak in the sights and sounds of a foreign yet familiar country, only to find yourself on a mad search for Skippy peanut butter and Fruit Loops to still their picky souls.

Hence our culinary tour of every fast-food restaurant in Israel. Granted, my husband and I were every bit as eager as our kids to taste from what is forbidden fruit to us in the United States. We did our own family taste tests, rating McDonald's against Burger King; Kentucky Fried Chicken against Pizza Hut. We planned our days around which hamburger joint to visit; in between, we tried to squeeze in a religious shrine or a historical landmark.

While I laugh about it now, I must admit I found the whole phenomenon somewhat unsettling. Not so much because of my kids, but because of me. I had not been in Israel in five years, and it has changed. By now, it has become a cliche to note that McDonald's is almost as ubiquitous in Israel as it is in America, and all that that supposedly represents: the "Americanization" of the Holy Land, the globalization of the uniquely Jewish state.

And yes, as an old-style Zionist — you know, the kind that romances the land, but never actually quite moves there — it felt vaguely "unkosher" to be eating a kosher Big Mac in an

American-style mall in the heart of Israel. You were supposed to come to Israel to work the land and help the desert bloom, right? And if you weren't the agricultural type, then at least you'd be inspired by the Western Wall, the ancient hills of Judea, the fortress at Masada. Not by the sight of a soldier, on his cell phone, tapping out a message on his hand-held computer, or by my nieces rushing home from school to pop a Disney video into the VCR.

But, on the other hand, maybe that is just the point. The modern State of Israel has in fact made the desert bloom — up from nowhere rise high-tech parks along the road near Herzliya and Kfar Saba, glass-enclosed office buildings bearing the names of home-grown Internet powerhouses. Peace and prosperity have come to this ancient land in enough measure to allay the skittishness of global corporations, who have invested in Israel and whose products appear throughout the land. And it was, after all, a kosher McDonald's in which we ate — still an experience unique to Israel.

I must admit that my point of reference when I'm in Israel is not the early days of the *chalutzim*, but rather with my own earlier visits, particularly the year that I spent in yeshiva after graduating from high school. Granted, that was 20 years ago (yikes!). But on those trips, Israel was truly the Holy Land. Be it on my teen tours or my year of study or my subsequent shorter trips, I was immersed in a world of students, of Torah, of idealism. Every step I took, be it on my way to a class or on a hike outside Jerusalem, seemed sanctified.

Now, when I visit my friends and family who live there, they are immersed in the same day-to-day activities that I am in America — working, raising a family, going grocery shopping. And so is the country as a whole. It is not just a holy enterprise.

But that is still at its core. I re-learned that on this trip, in between the visits to the amusement park and the Carvels, in ways that I had never previously experienced. Yes, the highlight was watching my son stick his first *"kvitel"* in the crevices of the Western Wall. And the initial sight of Jerusalem from the road from the airport still made my heart jump to my throat.

But there was also the magic of watching my kids play freely on the boardwalk along the Tel Aviv beach while some 70-something, European-bred Israelis, who most likely remember Tel Aviv as a sand dune, argued politics beside them. And there was much to take heart from the guy who runs the falafel stand near my brother-in-law's house who, when he realized he couldn't break my 100-shekel note, told me to give him the money another time. "Don't worry. I know you'll be back," he said.

I marveled at how seamlessly, though not without controversy and conflict, most of Israel moves between the sacred and the secular, the holy and the mundane. In this season of holidays, when many of us make the same type of transition from our workaday lives to a new Yontif every weekend, we are reminded constantly of the sanctity of time, of how we can transform an ordinary weekday into a Yom Kippur or a regular Sunday into Simchat Torah.

Israel reminded me of the sanctity of place. Even in its modern incarnation, Israel is the only place in the world where going to the supermarket still rises to the level of an act of faith, where taking a walk fulfills a commandment, and where, as my son remarked, "even the Burger King is in Hebrew!"

My Own Y2K Problem

December 1999

The drought. John F. Kennedy Jr. Encephalitis. Hurricane Floyd. Earthquakes in Turkey. Mudslides in Mexico. EgyptAir Flight 990. A 27-year-old woman getting hit on the head with a brick.

It's almost enough to make you believe in the Y2K bug — you know, the fear of the great unknown, not to mention the concern that all the lights will go out.

These past few months seem to have borne more than their fair share of natural and unnatural disasters around the world. Or is it no more than usual, and I'm just noticing these things more?

Maybe it comes with age. The older you get, the more you hear about tragedy and pain, close to home and farther away. Too many plane crashes; too many weird, disastrous weather patterns; too many of my peers being diagnosed with breast cancer; too many divorces; too many children developing rare illnesses. Every time I hear one of these tales, it is like another wound being inflicted, another reason to question the point of it all.

Sometimes I think it has to do with being a parent, this tendency to feel others' pain more acutely. For two solid weeks in April, I cried every time those horrific scenes from Colombine High School were replayed over and over on the television screen. And those scenes from the Jewish Community Center in Los Angeles? Forget about it. I found myself almost agreeing with George W. Bush, of all people, when he said that an evil is lurking in America.

Clearly, I have no answers to these fundamental questions. Why bad things happen to good people is a theological question older than the millennium itself.

I joke that there's more of this stuff going on now because of this Y2K bug sweeping the country. But as a practicing Jew, I'm not supposed to believe in any of that, right? Of what significance is the year 2000 to a truly committed Jew, after all?

I don't take this distinction lightly. Do you think it's merely coincidence that New Year's Eve falls on Friday night this year and Chanukah falls nowhere near Christmas? Don't you think God is trying to point something out to us? The calendar is conspiring to remind us that this is not our holiday, not our season, not even our millennium.

I remember so vividly being 16 and on vacation in Florida when New Year's Eve fell, tragically, it seemed to us, on a Friday night. A bunch of us partying wannabes sat around our hotel lobby bemoaning the fact that we couldn't do anything fun that night. One forward-looking young man went so far as to figure out that in the year 1999 — just when the new millennium would begin — New Year's Eve would again fall on Friday night. I remember being seriously bummed.

Then somebody pointed out that we'd all be nearly 40 at that point and we'd be such old geezers that we wouldn't even care.

I'm happy to report that that young prophet was right, mostly. I'll admit I wouldn't have minded being able to watch some of the festivities on television or getting together with some friends. But instead, I will probably spend New Year's Eve the way I spend most Friday nights — with my family, at our only sane and leisurely dinner of the week.

And for that I am glad. Because with all my questioning of senseless tragedy, for all my sense of foreboding and concern, this is the closest I'll ever come to an answer. I draw strength and sustenance from my family Shabbat dinners in ways that no New Year's Eve party could ever come near. It is my time to catch up with my husband and children, with a spirituality that is missing for most of the rest of the week and with a sense of stability and continuity that is hard to find in this terribly turbulent world.

When I was at a low point recently, after one or another mini or major disaster, I called the person I know who has weathered perhaps the worst storms life can offer and has managed, against all odds, to still look forward to another day. I called my father, the Holocaust survivor. He told me, as I knew he would, not to worry so much, things will work out.

"With all the tragedy you have endured and witnessed, how can you go on believing that things will be all right, that good things are yet to come?" I asked my father. "And how did you manage all these years to keep on going, building a life, a family, a future?"

This was not the first time this century that I have asked my father such things. But I'm a parent now, and he had a different answer. "Go upstairs to your children," who were then sound asleep, he advised me. "Take a look at them. And then you will know that it will be all right."

That's been his secret. And on this Friday morning, *erev* Shabbat, and *erev* the first night of Chanukah, I will share it with you. I even hope to carry it with me into the new millennium.

My Son and Joe

September 2000

The night Vice President Gore picked Sen. Joe Lieberman as his running mate, I committed a cardinal sin of parenthood. I roused my nine-year-old son from bed and brought him over to the TV.

"This is a night I want you to remember for the rest of your life," I told him, as the evening news went over the announcement from every angle. "This is the night that every Jewish mother could finally turn to her son or daughter and say, 'you too could one day become president of the United States.'"

After explaining who Lieberman was and why this day was so historic, my son's only question was, "So why isn't he wearing a yarmulke?"

All right. That's another story.

But that's not the point. My son didn't even realize that he was not supposed to aspire to the presidency until that night. He lives in a time and place where adults and children all around him are able to do just about anything they set their sights on. It's true that most of his baseball heroes are not Jewish, but he knows the name of every Jewish player that ever lived and assumes that most Jews just choose not to enter the Major Leagues.

But all the professions are open to him; any school he could dream of going to would take him, provided he had the grades; any artistic or creative talent he had could be duly cultivated and developed. He did not know that there were any limitations to his dreams.

But I did. Oh, it's not that I actively harbored a hope that my son would one day become president of the United States.

I'm not sure I would wish that job on anyone, let alone a child of mine. But somehow, I knew that as free and tolerated as we are in this country, there were unwritten rules, unmarked borders past which we dared not go.

And suddenly, when I saw Joe Lieberman standing up there beside the scion of one of Washington's elite political dynasties, I felt that we had crossed one of the final frontiers.

Now, others may see me as naive. Certainly members of my parents' generation — my parents included —a re still wary about the selection of Lieberman. All the latent anti-Semitism in this country, they argue, is going to come out in this election, in ugly charges during the campaign and, most persuasively, at the voting booth in November. Some of this has already begun to surface, and more is likely. They are also concerned that should things go badly for a Gore-Lieberman administration, somehow, the Jews will be blamed.

I do not discount this view, especially since it is shaped, at least in part, by the experiences of my parents' generation. The Holocaust will forever stand as testament to the ability of a "civilized" and "progressive" society to turn against Jews in the most horrific ways. The Shoah is also the strongest argument against getting too comfortable in the Diaspora.

Even in America, just a generation ago, Jews were inclined not to be too Jewish in public. Observant men, as a rule, did not wear kipas in the street, and even traditional families — like Lieberman's — sent their children to public schools and gave them names that helped them blend in with the rest of America. Ultimately, this is not our country and these are not our people.

I understand all of this. And yet. And yet there's Joe Lieberman nominated for vice president. I am a member of a different generation and I have never experienced anti-Semitism firsthand. So I can hope and I can believe. And I can't help but look at the nomination of Lieberman as one of the proudest days ever for Jews in America. Here was a Jew — an observant Jew, no less — who, without compromising his principles, has led a life of exemplary public service and was chosen to help lead a national ticket purely on the basis of his accomplishments.

And I actually know people who know the person who may become vice president of the United States! They've *davened* with him in shul, or sent their kids to the same camp as he sent his, or joined him in walking to Capitol Hill to cast an important vote on Shabbat. It's like the ultimate game of Jewish geography.

The point is he's one of us. What he juggles in the Senate is a more public and high-stakes version of what many of us do every day in our own, more private lives. Wouldn't it be an amazing feeling to know that every time you head out the door of your office early on a Friday in the winter, you'd know the vice president of the United States was doing the same thing?

His commitment to public service came out of his commitment to Judaism, and his religious observance informs his public service, most notably in his moral critique of President Clinton in the wake of the Lewinsky affair that has earned him national recognition. He is, in my opinion, a walking *kiddush Hashem*, someone who brings dignity and glory to the name of God and our way of life. And besides inspiring us in our Jewish observance, he may also inspire more of us to participate in public life, which too few of us really do.

Not every Jew will agree with his politics, and, in the end, of course, the Gore-Lieberman ticket may very well lose. But one of the two major parties in this country has put him forward as the man to help lead this country at the start of the new century. And now I can honestly turn to my son and say — there is nothing to which you cannot aspire.

Mothers, Sons and Guns

November 2000

The most disturbing image to come out of Israel in recent weeks was a photograph that ran last week in *The New York Times*. No, not the picture of the bloodied American yeshiva student whom the *Times* and other papers wrongly identified as a Palestinian. And not the photo of the lynched soldier being thrown out of a window by a Palestinian mob. These were, of course, wrenching.

But the photo I refer to was, for me, more unsettling and ultimately more insidious. It showed a group of four young-to-middle-aged Israeli women, with long skirts and hair covered, learning how to use a gun. Their faces wore a look of intense concentration mixed with abject horror. No doubt mothers all, they could have passed easily for members of my shul or neighbors in my community. But I live here and they live in Jerusalem, and so I drive my kids to soccer while they learn how to handle a gun.

"I was so against, screaming against, guns," one woman, an American immigrant, told the *Times*. "And now look at me."

I became a supporter of the peace process as an outgrowth of being a mother. My second son was born in the fall of 1993, just as Oslo entered our vocabulary not as a city in Norway but as the symbol of hope for peace in the Middle East.

Not long after his birth, I was on the phone with my husband's aunt, who fought in the War of Independence and watched three sons don uniforms in defense of the state, joking about our families giving birth only to sons.

Or, at least, I was joking. To her, there was nothing funny about bearing sons. "You are lucky you live in America," she said. "Here, it is so hard to have sons. Sons become soldiers."

So what's so terrible about yearning not to live like that anymore? How could anyone begrudge the mothers and fathers, wives, sisters, and girlfriends, who no longer wanted to send their boys off to war?

And boys so many of them are; my brother-in-law is a psychiatrist who, on reserve duty in the vaunted Israel Defense Forces, treats soldiers for bed-wetting and other signs of nervous tension. Was it any coincidence that the leaders in the fight for peace, Yitzhak Rabin and Ehud Barak, were past generals, who had seen for themselves the fruits of war?

And what of the constant fear of terrorist attacks, that can strike at any moment and do not discriminate among men and women, old and young? How long could a people go on living like that? Peace with the Palestinians, even if not philosophically palatable, seemed at least like the only way to live a life. "*V'chai bahem*," the Torah tells us; you should live by them, by these commandments. We are told to choose life; what good is it to fight for every corner of land, if so many of our sons have to die in the process?

There is no doubt that Oslo has helped. In the last seven years, Israel has palpably relaxed. The economy, as we all know, has been booming; the great issues of the day have been social and religious in nature, rather than military; and people were already commenting that it was getting too easy to get out of army duty because the army didn't need all those recruits anymore.

When I was in Israel last summer, after an absence of five years, what impressed me most was how normal the country had gotten — for good and for ill. I took the ubiquitous Mc-

Donald's restaurants as a sign that Israel had finally arrived as a member in good standing of the global economy.

And now this. Like so many other supporters of the peace process, I have been stopped dead in my tracks. Our "partners in peace" beat two Russian reservists to death and flung them out the window like trash, chanting in triumph all the while. "We have been duped by a seven-year ruse," writes a friend from Jerusalem, a former believer in the peace process whose son now travels to school in an armored van.

And so I yield to the right wing on these points. You were right about the depth of our antagonists' enmity. You were right about Arafat, right about the Palestinians' intentions. They have surely betrayed those who put their trust in them.

But this does not mean that we should betray ourselves. I will not yield on the ultimate pursuit of peace — though it may have to wait, though it may take some other form, the nature of which I cannot yet begin to imagine.

What is left to us otherwise? Only an endless cycle of hatred and violence and fear and death. This is not a way to live. In the natural order of things, women who wear long skirts and cover their hair should not be toting guns. And mothers should not be burying their sons. And we, the Jewish people, should not be so filled with hate.

A Measure of Redemption

April 2001

Last month I attended my first-grader's siddur party. For anyone familiar with this ceremony, the mention of it usually brings a sentimental smile. It is a mainstay of the Jewish day school experience, and marks a child's first milestone on his or her road to acquiring the skills necessary to becoming a literate and practicing Jew.

In my kids' school, the ceremony is given great pageantry. Children are dressed in their finest, parents and other family members are in attendance, and after a brief performance by the children, the principal himself presents each child with his or her first prayer book with their name spelled out in calligraphy on a beautiful cover. A party, complete with cake and candy, follows.

At its heart, the ritual is simple and sweet, and most likely derives from the even older tradition — still carried on in many chasidic communities today — of giving young boys a taste of honey as they prepare to learn the aleph bet for the first time. There is something that we Jews think is lovely about our children acquiring the building blocks of their faith, and of carrying on the traditions of their forebears.

If I can borrow a friend's description of herself, I am an absolute mushball at these kinds of events. The tears begin to well up as soon as the kids enter stage left, and I can't stop the flow until well after I have driven home. Now I admit I'm the kind of mother who gets misty-eyed at only the slightest provocation; I can get choked up watching my daughter play peacefully with her dollhouse.

But these ceremonies that mark the passing of the torch, the continuity of our people and of my family — these just send me over the top. Always, I think, the tears derive from the same source. Always, there is the sense of wonder that I, the granddaughter of devout Jews murdered by Hitler, the daughter of parents who have suffered so much — here I am raising my children amid comfort and lack of fear, and raising them as Jews, in a way that my parents and even my grandparents might be proud.

The relative normalcy of my existence and that of my children's, compared to those of my parents and grandparents, constantly amazes me, and humbles me.

Just the other day, while driving home from a wonderful family bat mitzvah, my parents talked about another, distant relative who died a while back. "Did he and his wife have any children?" I asked, just out of curiosity. "They each lost their children in the war," my mother replied, almost matter-of-factly. "This was a second marriage for both of them and they decided not to have any more children." This was almost casual conversation, mind you, and it left me devastated.

What came before us, and what was lost, is mind-boggling. Sometimes I feel I've gotten my arms around it; then my mother makes an aside like that, and reminds me all over again how little I can actually grasp of the unspeakable horror of it all.

I write all this as Passover is upon us. It is a holiday that no two families practice exactly alike and yet it is one that unites us all like no other. We have each developed our own traditions at the seder; the most fortunate among us are able to have these traditions passed down through the generations.

At my family's seder, the tradition that always stood out was the pause we all took at the passage, "In every generation, it is incumbent on every person to see himself as if he himself were delivered from Egypt." Then my father would talk of his experiences in the Holocaust, always noting that the first seder night is the anniversary of the Warsaw Ghetto Uprising, which began on April 19, 1943. And so for me, the holiday of redemption is forever associated with a very real bondage.

Recently, a book was published by the U.S. Holocaust Memorial Museum, *Life Reborn: Jewish Displaced Persons 1945-1951*. It recounts the extraordinary tales of how shattered people picked up the shards of their lives and, against all odds, built new lives for themselves and subsequently for their children. It was, at best, a bittersweet redemption for many of them.

Years later, many of these survivors, including my father, can sit down for their Passover seders with their children and grandchildren gathered around them. That in itself is another kind of redemption.

And then there is my son's siddur party. When my son so proudly reached out to take hold of his new siddur, unbeknownst to him, he was reaching back through the generations. He will learn to pray using the same words that his great-grandfathers used before him. And he will pray out loud, without shame and without fear. Let us all join with him at our seder tables. If true redemption is possible, it lies therein.

Toward Redemption: a Poland Diary

August 2001

Day One: My flight was delayed for six hours, so I am greeted at the Warsaw airport by my friend, Naomi, and our Polish tour guide with the news that we are going straight to Treblinka. This is as fitting a way to begin my journey as any, I suppose. It is here that my grandfather and aunt met their deaths, along with nearly one million other Jews (my grandmother died in the ghetto).

There is nothing left of Treblinka; the Germans destroyed it before the war ended. A visitor today confronts a train track, a large clearing in the woods and 18,000 stones of varying sizes, representing the Jewish communities that were wiped out during the war. Here, beside the rather large stone bearing the name of my father's hometown, Czestochowa, I shed the first of my many tears in Poland. Poland is a country drowning in Jewish tears.

This was the closest I would ever come to my family's gravesite. I recite some Psalms, place a small rock on top of the large stone, and look up at the appropriately overcast sky. "I am here!" I cry to my grandfather's spirit. I mean it in the literal sense: I have returned to this land, to his birthplace and burial place, to retrace my father's steps, and perhaps, in some way, find my own.

But I am here also in the existential sense: I am alive, which is more than you, my grandfather, might ever have hoped for. Your son survived this horrific war, he built a family, and he raised us as proud and practicing Jews. I am your granddaughter, I am here, and maybe there is some vindication in that.

Day Two: We visit the various monuments that mark the sites of the famed Warsaw Ghetto, of which nothing remains: the Umshlagplatz, where Jews were gathered and deported, mostly to Treblinka; the Mila 18 bunker where the leaders of the Warsaw Ghetto Uprising eventually died; the ancient Jewish cemetery.

Then we visit the small town where Naomi's father lived, and actually find what we believe to be his house. The current residents never heard Naomi's family name before and were sure the house was built in the 1970s.

Their next-door neighbor tells us, unsolicited, how her father tried to help the Jews during the war, but they betrayed him. When we leave to return to our car, the windows to the house are all shuttered, the door bolted, and the grandparents, no doubt of the war generation, are standing guard, arms clasped, smiles gone.

Day Three: Finally, Czestochowa. I have heard so much about this small city over the years that I cannot believe it is a physical reality. I have come to Poland specifically to walk these streets, to hear what they will whisper to me about who I am, where I am come from, perhaps even where I should go from here.

Instead, once again, I am confronted with a plaque. Everywhere I go in Poland, there is a plaque. Here a plaque noting where a synagogue once stood. There a plaque in memory of the 42 Jews murdered in "anti-Semitic riots" in Kielce in 1946, a year after the war ended. And this, on an outside wall of the hospital where my father was born: "The hospital was built in the years 1909-1913 on the initiative of the Jewish Charity Society and the Jewish community of Czestochowa. During the

German occupation, 1939-1945, the staff and doctors of the hospital with few exceptions were murdered by the Nazis."

There is a breathtaking simplicity to these plaques, a matter-of-factness that begins to wear me down after a few days. I could close my eyes in my father's hometown and see, as he described it, the thousands of Jews pouring out into the streets on a Shabbat afternoon, the kids running around, the adults *"shpatzeering"* in their finery along the boulevard, all the shops closed for the holiday. When I open my eyes, all I see is a plaque.

And if I have any doubt as to the significance of the plaques to Poles today, when I try to enter the courtyard of the building where my father grew up, I was chased out by a group of Poles, who cursed and screamed at us as we headed back to our car. One old lady followed us out, and when told what we were looking for, said, yes, the Jews were here once, but they went away.

Over there, across the street, though, was one of their schools. And down the road a bit stood one of their churches. But the Jews themselves, they went away.

Day Four: Auschwitz. This is where they went. I cannot even describe this place. It is the abyss, and I have stood on its edge. The millions who passed through this hell still cry out from this earth; we can still find shards of bone in the ground, not to mention the floor-to-ceiling mounds of shoes, suitcases, and baby clothes that lay piled up in some of the former barracks here. The sheer organizational skill put into running this place is overwhelming.

The huge black-and-white photographs, taken while the camp was in operation, stand at various points about the grounds, leaving very little to the imagination. Will I ever be able to erase the picture of the three children, no doubt siblings, around the same ages as my own kids, holding hands, eyes wide and terrified, marching bewildered to their deaths?

Day Five: Krakow. Finally, some signs of Jewish life. Shuls that are still standing from the 14th and 15th Centuries. The famed Remu synagogue, where services are once again being held on Shabbat. The square in the heart of the old Jewish quarter, beautifully restored. Our hotel on the square is called the "Ester." Across the street is the "Eden" and down the block is the "Klezmer House." Aptly, Naomi calls it a Jewish Disneyland. The facades look real, but there is nothing substantive behind them. For there are no Jews in Poland today, only plaques and gravesites. The venerable cemeteries, ironically, serve in many towns as the only reminders that Jewish life flourished in this land for centuries.

Day Six, Shabbat: Krakow again. A huge soundstage, replete with man-sized speakers and strobe lighting, is being set up on this central square. Where once Jews poured out of a dozen synagogues on Shabbat morning, filling this square, and where they were once herded like animals to a nearby ghetto and then eventually to their deaths—this square will now be host to the gala concert culminating the week-long Eleventh Annual Jewish Festival of Krakow.

At about 6 p.m., a band of klezmer musicians, replete with Bukharan yarmulkes and embroidered shirts, steps onto the stage and the crowd, which had been gathering all afternoon, goes wild. The crowd, of course, is 99 percent Polish. Only the performers and a relative handful of tourists are Jewish. Again, the question goes begging: Where are the Jews?

And what to make of this spectacle? On the one hand, here is Jewish music ringing out in the streets of Krakow for the first time in more than 60 years. On the other hand, I tend to think that the murdered Jews of Krakow are turning over in their graves.

Day Seven: Return home. My feelings of redemption and vindication, with which I started my trip, have all but dissipated. Yes, I am here, I cried to my grandfather. But so many millions are not. There is no redemption in retracing my forebears' footsteps, only to arrive in Treblinka. And there is no vindication in returning to my father's town, only to be chased out again.

There is only despair. And many unanswered, and unanswerable, questions. Hitler may not have succeeded in vanquishing the Jewish people. But he did manage to wipe out a civilization. Poland, where Jews had lived for nearly a thousand years, where Jewish life was rich in shuls and schools and community organizations, where great rabbinic scholars emerged alongside iconic Jewish cultural figures, where more than a dozen Yiddish newspapers vied for readers on the streets of Warsaw, where over three million Jews lived before the war: This Poland is today *Judenrein*, devoid of Jews and Jewish life. It is one large Jewish cemetery.

And I, the daughter and granddaughter of this tortured heritage, rush home to embrace my children. And to pray that somehow, this way lies redemption.

What We Lost

October 2001

As the daughter of a Holocaust survivor, as someone who visited Auschwitz just this past summer, as the close relative of many loved ones living in Israel, you'd think I might have learned a thing or two. That the future is at best unpredictable. That horrible things happen to very, very good people. That life is fragile and insecure and by no means a sure thing.

And yet until September 11, I'm not sure I ever really internalized those truisms. I lived in a cocoon perhaps of my own making, born of my life experiences, that allowed me to believe that life would be fairly predictable and secure. Be a decent and upright person, work hard, be kind to friends and family and, with a little luck and faith in God, things will work out.

I realized, of course, that people get sick and die, that illness could strike or some horrible accident could occur and a precious life might be lost. These events are invariably tragic, but they do not change the course of daily life or the very fabric of society.

"*Der mensch tracht and Got lacht*" — man thinks, or plans, and God laughs. This Yiddish saying, so obvious to the European Jews who authored it, keeps coming into my head lately. Where did I come off thinking that life would always be a function of what I wanted it to be? How could I walk the streets of my father's beloved hometown in Poland, a town he never really wanted to leave, and not realize that dreams can be shattered in an instant?

How could I look at pictures of children on their way to the crematoria and not know that pure evil exists in this world and has done its work before?

Somehow, I thought that was all behind us. I thought we had vanquished evil in 1945, and that the children and grandchildren of those who survived would be spared further tragedy.

I recently read an essay by the father of a 15-year-old girl who was severely injured in the Sbarro bombing in Jerusalem this summer. He is the son of a Holocaust survivor who came of age, like I did, in an era of relative peace and prosperity. "My friends and I, the generation of Israel's revival, have already sensed the light at the end of the tunnel, the vision of peace and humanity at our doorstep," he writes.

And here was his daughter, her body riddled with "nails, bolts and screws," lying in a hospital bed and asking about the children ahead of her on line at the pizza shop who had been burning before her eyes. "I understand now that the images of flames and smoke, the voices crying out 'Shema Yisrael,' were heard by two generations in my family — my father's and my daughter's." He himself, he writes, had been lulled into a false sense of hope for a lasting peace.

Having been thankfully spared any direct loss from the attack on the World Trade Center, I have suffered, like so many others, a more indirect loss. It is a loss in a belief that the future will be better than the past, that my children's lives will be better than my own. It is a loss of a sense of security, of a sureness in my step, of a confidence in my surroundings.

We had friends visiting from Israel this summer; the parents are American-born, and their kids have been here many times. This is the first time, however, that they all remarked, with a tinge of jealousy, on how carefree and easy life was in America. You didn't have to figure out what road to drive down in order not to get shot at; you didn't have to decide, on a life-or-death basis, whether to go out for dinner; you didn't have to jump every time you heard a siren.

I felt too guilt-stricken to suggest that perhaps they might want to come to America for a while, as others had, just to get away from the tension and anxiety. And yes, I was thankful that I did not have to live like that and my children did not have to grow up with those fears.

Now, of course, my smugness has been stripped away. America is no longer a safe haven. As a friend of mine said the other day, if we're going to live like this, we might as well live in Israel. At least there one has a sense of a greater cause.

But as in so many other ways, we American Jews can learn much from our Israeli brothers and sisters. Despite their well-grounded fears and bitter experience, they get up every morning and go to work and send their children to school. They get married, they have babies, they make birthday parties for their kids, they are even in the middle of making Sukkot. My cousin in Israel just got married, and after some trepidation, decided to come to New York for her honeymoon after all!

Life goes on, as it must. In some ways, with our priorities suddenly set in order for us, life goes on in even sharper relief than before. We are all, perhaps, being kinder to one another, reaching out more to those in need, drawing closer to our loved ones. Yes, I am hugging my children even tighter now. And praying, still praying, that they grow up never really understanding why.

The Glory Of The Mundane

December 2001

My car radio is still tuned to the all-news station that I happened to turn to at 8:48 a.m. on September 11 just to get the traffic report. Normally, I listened to music in the car. I stayed with that station throughout that horrific day as I painstakingly navigated my way home. Now, I can't seem to turn it off. All news, all the time.

But at home, my television is no longer fixed on CNN. I have gone back to the "West Wing" and "ER," where I can watch my political crises and medical emergencies from the safe distance of fiction.

I still have not taken my children to any place in Manhattan that might attract a crowd, including their favorite museums or the Thanksgiving Day Parade. Sunday afternoons were rarely left unplanned; I was always taking my kids to some activity or another. Now, I hang out around the house or find diversions close to home.

But I have gone back to work, and each day, I drive over the George Washington Bridge and plunge into Midtown. I've even gotten to the point where I no longer take a deep breath and say a quick prayer as we head over the bridge.

I still grab the newspaper obsessively each morning. I need to make sure the world is still standing, that no other major catastrophe has occurred while I was sleeping. But once I ascertain that it is safe to go outside, I no longer feel the need to read every word of the "Nation Challenged" section. I can turn, albeit somewhat sheepishly, to other news, to my professional interests in the business section, and even, on Sundays, to the completely diversionary Styles section. It's the little pleasures, after all, that make the difference.

So my world is the same, and yet not the same as it was before September 11. It seemed to me, back in the dark days of September, that my life and that of those around me could never return to what we used to call normal. How could I ever again worry about what to make for dinner when the world was coming to an end? How could I focus on my job, on my kids' homework, on all the daily, mundane tasks of life when our very survival was at stake?

And, in some ways, this perspective still holds. I am more fearful now in my surroundings and more circumspect in making plans. The future too seems much less certain, and I worry particularly about the world in which my children will come of age. Will their prospects be as bright as mine were when I set out on adulthood? Will their dreams and ambitions necessarily be more circumscribed? Will they even, God forbid, still be living in a time of unending war against an elusive enemy?

But while dark clouds still hang over us, and the fear will not go away, I feel that we are coming out of a period of shock and mourning. Of course, for those who lost loved ones in the attacks, life will never be the same again. But for most of the rest of us, the rhythms of our lives have picked up largely where they left off on September 10. I am back to focusing on homework, my job, and the tugs of community involvement. I can get annoyed about my dishwasher that refuses to clean my dishes, and take pleasure in a fun movie. And I can begin to plan, however tentatively, a family vacation in the coming months.

But September 11 has undoubtedly refocused my priorities. It is exactly those daily, mundane tasks that I cherish most. I have found new joy in old routines; never before have I taken such pleasure in preparing meals for my family, in seeing my kids fly off the bus from school, loudly arguing or complaining about school, in making myself the same cup of tea each morning at work. I have always found a special blessedness in Friday night dinners with my family; now I don't even mind cleaning up afterwards.

Chanukah arrives this week with its bright light of hope and miracle. On the one hand, it often gets caught up in the spirit of the season that permeates America this time of year. But at the same time, it serves as a potent reminder that, as much as we share with our fellow Americans, particularly this year, we are still apart. As Americans, we are regrouping after September 11. But in Israel, the pain doesn't stop. It doesn't let up. There is no time to catch your breath and return to some semblance of normalcy.

I write this column just after hearing about the latest tragedy to strike in the heart of Jerusalem. I'm not quite sure in what spirit to light the candles this year. Perhaps in the spirit of hope, in the spirit of triumph over adversity, in the spirit of trying to carry on. Perhaps, too, with a prayer that someday soon all Jews will be able to hug their families tight and bask in the glory of the mundane.

Rightward Bound

May 2002

Somewhere around the Passover massacre in Netanya, I took a sharp turn to the right and morphed into my father.

My father is a Holocaust survivor, someone who has experienced first-hand the worst that the world has to offer Jews. Politically, he stands somewhere to the right of Arik Sharon. He voted for Bush and Giuliani and D'Amato, anyone he deemed a staunch friend of the Jews. He couldn't stand President Clinton and likes his wife even less.

As for Arafat, my father didn't trust him for one minute, and opposed the Oslo Accords and the peace process from the outset. Arafat would never be satisfied with just the West Bank and Gaza, my father insisted. He wants nothing less than the entire State of Israel. And when it came to Germany and the rest of Europe — let's just say he was not in the least surprised when a synagogue was recently torched in France or when Berliners took to the streets to protest the Israeli actions in Jenin and Ramallah.

I, perhaps predictably, have argued with him every step of the way. As soon as I was old enough to vote, I became a registered Democrat. Not only did I vote for Clinton and Gore, but I did so enthusiastically. The nomination of Joe Lieberman for vice president just put me over the top. I even disliked Giuliani's attitude and his politics.

As for Arafat, I did trust him — or rather, I trusted that he would act in his own best interest and finally make peace with Israel. I supported the Oslo Accords and believed wholeheartedly that the best thing for Israel was to give up land if it meant that we would finally have peace. The last time I was in

Israel, which was in 1999, I felt I was witnessing the real fruits of the peace process — the sense of normalcy, the prosperity, the feelings of good will that seemed to pervade the country at the time.

And when it comes to Germany and the rest of Europe, while I am too much my father's daughter ever to have forgiven what they did, I was willing to believe that a new generation would bring about a new day in Europe. My father could never put the Holocaust behind him, but certainly my generation and that of my children's were allowed to move on, while not forgetting the past. The future, after all, had to be better than the past. Otherwise, what was the point?

Now I wonder. Maybe it's creeping middle age, or maybe it's a confluence of world and personal events that have made me much more pessimistic, but I find myself increasingly mouthing my father's lines. Not consciously, of course. It's not that I woke up one morning and decided my father was right all along. But recent events have forced me to reach certain conclusions that I have resisted for many years.

In reading all the press coverage of the Middle East, I am startled to find myself agreeing not only with the Bush administration, but with its most hard-line members. I hear myself, in shock, talk about anti-Semitism in Europe as something almost genetic, in the bones, in a land so drenched in our blood. And as for Arafat, at first I felt betrayed. Now I feel actual hate toward him and his henchmen.

None of these new sentiments makes me feel very good. I do not wear right-wing clothing comfortably. I still recoil from associating with the likes of Gary Bauer and Alan Keyes and the Christian Coalition, and yet they are emerging as the most stalwart supporters of Israel in a world that suddenly seems so hostile to Jews. Where is an old-fashioned liberal to turn?

In these very pages last week, someone from Birmingham, England, took the time and effort to write to a Jewish newspaper in New York to tell its readers that "the Jews are no better than the Nazis and I hope most people in the world now turn against you for the way you are behaving." This from a country I considered a bastion of civilization, that led the fight against those very Nazis half a century ago.

In a world gone mad, at least since September 11, we are all being called upon to uphold and protect what is most important to us. Many of my assumptions and beliefs have been turned on their head in the past few months. But I know some things for sure: I believe fervently in peace; I value human life, and Jewish life, far more than I value land. What we are facing now, however, is a struggle for our very existence and for the future of our people.

We are not the first Jews to wage this fight, nor, I'm afraid, will we be the last. Welcome to Jewish history, my friends. Let's hope our children will be able to write a better chapter.

Mid-life Aliyah

August 2003

We have friends making aliyah this summer. In many ways, their lives until now have not been all that different from ours. They are Modern Orthodox professionals in their early 40s, they have five children ranging in age from four to thirteen, they live in the same suburban community as we do, and they are neither rich nor poor.

In fact, until they announced their aliyah plans several months ago, they seemed, like most of the rest of us, to be well rooted right where they were. They even built an addition to their house not long ago. They were heavily involved in their children's school and active members of their synagogue. All their extended family lives here in the United States. Of course, they were ardent Zionists and great supporters of Israel, but hey, aren't we all? There was no reason to suspect that they would actually switch gears in the middle of a well-worn path and embark on a whole new journey. I mean, people are entitled to a mid-life crisis, but doesn't that usually involve buying a sportier car?

And yet, for our friends, this move represents picking up where they left off years ago. "This is a lifelong dream," says the female half of the couple. "Certainly, at times I thought, 'this [life in America] is it.' When we talked about the future, it was here. But if pressed, 'where do you see yourself in 10 years?' I wouldn't have said here. [Aliyah] never left my mind."

And so the question of course: why now? The question really is twofold. Why uproot themselves now, when they are settled in their community, secure in their jobs, and in the middle of raising their children in a comfortable environment? And why now, when the Intifada rages on in Israel and the economy there is in the dumps?

Ironically, for this couple, it was the Intifada that actually pushed them toward Israel, not away. They watched the escalating violence from afar, feeling more and more that their place was there, not here. "We felt guilty about being here," says our friend. She recalls her husband returning from shul one Shabbat two years ago, citing a passage from the Torah portion that we just happened to have read again last week. It comes after representatives from the tribes of Reuven and Gad ask Moses to allow them to settle on land east of the Jordan River, while the rest of the nation proceeded to try to conquer Canaan. Moses responds: "Shall your brethren go to war, while you sit here?"

The question hit home, and out friends have been preparing to leave for Israel ever since. As to their station in life, they knew that the longer they stayed here, the harder it would get to leave. As settled as they were, they felt they had a window of opportunity now, while their kids were still young enough, to move without disrupting their lives too much.

I have always had the utmost respect for anyone going on aliyah, particularly those who leave the comforts of the United States simply out of love for Zion. I have a number of friends who did that fresh out of college, or when they were newly married. But now, 20 years later, when we all seem so set in our ways, when we are so caught up in our careers and communities, when our parents are aging and our children are growing — now seems like such a more difficult time to pick ourselves up and start all over again somewhere else.

Yet these friends are doing it. And it's not only them. They consider themselves fortunate because about a dozen other families in our community are making aliyah this summer, providing each other with support, advice, and encouragement.

Let's face it, most of us are not going to make aliyah at this point. But the example set by this couple and others like them is one we can all take to heart. Even in "middle age" — that vast wasteland of climbing up the career ladder and remodeling the kitchen — there is still occasion to take stock and see where you are vis a vis the values to which you subscribe and the goals you once set for yourself. Have we lost our way? Is this where we wanted to be?

"Life throws you curveballs," says another woman in our community, explaining why it took her and her husband nearly 20 years after falling in love with Israel to follow up with aliyah. Life indeed does do that. And for some imaginings of youth, it may in fact be too late. But if these families making aliyah at this stage in life teach us anything, it is not to give up on the dreams you hold most dear, however dormant they may seem. There really is no time like the present. Go ahead, reach for your dreams.

Lessons from Cape Canaveral

February 2003

As anyone who sends their kids to a Jewish day school knows, the advent of winter vacation in mid-January has less to do with avoiding the appearance of celebrating Christmas and more to do with cheap airfares to Florida. In fact, I believe the schools invented "yeshiva week" to allow every family to fulfill their obligation of taking their kids to Disney World without having to wait on long lines.

And so, last month, we dutifully flew to Orlando to do the Disney thing. But my kids, thank God, have interests outside of Mickey, and my oldest in particular pushed for us to go visit Cape Canaveral, a short drive from Orlando. My husband and I were annoyed at ourselves when we realized we missed the shuttle launch carrying the Israeli astronaut (I didn't even know his name at that point) by just a few days, but shuttle launches happen all the time, we figured. No big loss.

Cape Canaveral proved to be a great visit. For my husband and me, it was a trip down memory lane, watching the film of the first moon landing, walking through a mock-up of mission control from the 1960s, seeing the exhibits on the history of space exploration beginning in the 1950s. It was kind of sad, we noted, how the glory days of NASA were 30 years ago. What have they done for us lately?

My kids, on the other hand, were transfixed. My oldest, who is 11, ran from one exhibit to the next, excited by everything he saw. Last summer, he attended a local space camp run by NASA that simulates the astronauts' experiences, and he proudly carried his graduation certificate around Cape Canaveral with him, just in case anyone asked. His jaw dropped as he watched the film of Neil Armstrong taking his first steps on the moon. We climbed into a mock-up of the shuttle, and he imagined what it would be like to sleep in space and to pilot the controls. They even had daily briefings live from the shuttle, and videos around the room showed the astronauts as they orbited the Earth.

As the day went on, I began to see the Kennedy Space Center through his eyes, and I understood the great potential and limitless dreams that such a place could inspire. Like many of my generation, I had kind of forgotten about the space program. But this was the future, and I wanted my son to be a part of it. I was pleased that when we returned home, my son began to scour the newspaper each day looking for news about the shuttle. The day after we got home, he called one of his best friends, who had been to Cape Canaveral several times, and together they went over every detail.

And then, needless to say, disaster struck. Of course, we were all devastated. But my son was shell-shocked. He stayed up late with us Saturday night, watching the news reports in stunned silence. "I'm scared," he finally said before he went to bed. The next morning, he scanned the headlines in the paper and then wordlessly put the paper aside. That night, he tried reading one of his numerous science fiction books and just couldn't. For him, a new realization had dawned: space exploration is not just about glory and adventure. It's about human lives, it's about fragility and vulnerability, it's about dreams not always fulfilled.

This is the world in which we are raising our kids. Fly a rocket to outer space; it goes up in smoke. Send up the best and the brightest, men and women at the peak of their powers, and they come back to Earth as debris. Build the tallest buildings in the world, ones that touch the sky, and they come crumbling down in the blink of an eye. Is the lesson here one of hubris?

Are we, like the ancients who built the Tower of Babel, guilty of trying to reach for the Heavens?

And this doesn't even include the Jewish angle. Of all the shuttle launches in the last decade, when representatives from some thirty countries have flown on board, why was this the one that came crashing down? Why was it the shuttle carrying a painting from a child in Terezinstadt and a Torah scroll, not to mention the proud Jew who carried them aloft? Why, at a time of such anxiety and tragedy in Israel, was the one great symbol of hope and pride dashed to his death?

Must I teach my son to curb his dreams? As a Jew and as a citizen of Earth, must I tell him that the sky is indeed the limit? Truth is, I am learning right along with him. I was raised in an era when nothing seemed impossible, when my parents and teachers could instill in me — and believe it too — a sense that I could accomplish whatever I set out to do.

I am learning in my own life that that is not always true. And now, I must caution my children, as well. We can set out to reach for our dreams, but we may not always be able to realize them. What we can learn from people like Ilan Ramon, however, is that it is the reach that is most important. Ramon died doing exactly what he set out to do, and no doubt he has inspired countless others to pick up where he left off and fulfill his mission. Therein, ultimately, lies his greatness. We may not be able to achieve all our ambitions; this is the unfortunate truth. But that makes them no less worthy a goal, no less noble a dream.

Afterword

Come Together

Barry Lichtenberg

September 2004

Before my wife died last fall, I made a number of promises to her. One was that she would be buried in Israel. Another was that our three young children and I would spend time together in Israel over the summer. "You will need time to regroup," she explained. And so we arrived in Israel last month with my marching orders firmly in hand. Our agenda was perhaps overly ambitious for a two-week trip. Bring the children to their mother's final resting place. Celebrate a *hanahat* (donning of) tefillin ceremony for my eldest child, who turned 13 over the summer. Visit with friends and relatives. Have some family time. Regroup.

We went to Rifka's grave at the start of our visit, both because I could not wait and because I wanted it to be over. Rifka is interred on a wind-swept hill overlooking the Judean Hills in Har Menuhot, the vast necropolis on the outskirts of Jerusalem. I had been at her grave four months earlier, for the unveiling. But it was the first time for our children. When Rifka, on this page, first went public with her illness over two years ago, she wrote that "it takes a village" for a family to function with cancer in its midst. When Rifka left us, the village remained. Looking back on those desolate first weeks and months following Rifka's death, it was the myriad of large and small acts of kindness that kept us — and keeps us — going. High school kids helped with homework, adults with shopping. One weekend we went away and returned home to find our living and dining rooms painted. (Fortunately, the color

---

RIFKA ROSENWEIN

was neutral.)

Obviously, these measures do not fill the void, nor are they meant to. Rather, they demonstrate that we are not alone, that others are rooting for us to succeed. As a rabbi told me in Israel last month, "You can give up on God, but never give up on the Jews." I'm not sure I agree with him on either count, but I got the point.

We also need time alone. And so, every Friday evening, meal invitations are politely declined and my children and I dine at home. The Shabbat eve dinner had always been Rifka's favorite time, when we would come together and report on the week that was. It is at this meal that Rifka's absence is most viscerally felt. But this is how I want it to be, to keep Rifka a presence in our lives while learning to live without her.

In the end, it was my children who, at the cemetery, remained relatively composed and I who was reduced to sobs by the eulogies that my seven-year-old daughter and 10-year-old son spontaneously delivered. My eldest was unable to speak and recited Psalms instead. We lit a candle and left Jerusalem.

And we did "regroup." We swapped minivans with an Israeli family in the States for the summer and drove to the Northern Galilee for a few days. There we hiked under canopies of trees aside flowing brooks. We visited Yad Layeled, a museum designed for children that is devoted to the Holocaust's youngest victims. We ate at a tasty and tastefully designed Arab-owned kosher restaurant. A large mural on the wall recreated the now-famous photograph of the late Prime Minister Yitzhak Rabin lighting King Hussein's cigarette outside the Oval Office, a melancholy reminder of what might have been.

I was drawn back to Rifka's grave the day before the *hana-hat* tefillin. This time, my children begged off. If I was more composed the second time around, the solace that I sought still eluded me. I would not be returning to Rifka's grave for a while and I struggled for the appropriate thing to say or think or do.

The *hanahat* tefillin ceremony is rapidly becoming the latest addition to the Jewish lifecycle calendar, the opening event of the bar mitzvah Olympics. It typically takes place at morning services a few days or weeks before the young man's 13th birthday and marks his joining the company of tefillin-wearing adults. "Ceremony" is a misnomer; the event's wonder lies in its ordinariness as father helps son bind the tefillin to his arm, head, and hand.

In our version of the *hanahat* tefillin, we prayed at the Western Wall before the full heat of the day set in. The Wall's shadow provided temporary shelter from the blazing sun. As the sun rose and the shade diminished, our small congregation huddled closer and closer to the Wall. Following services, about 50 friends and relatives joined us for brunch at a restaurant overlooking the Old City walls. Afterward, the bar mitzvah boy performed on a piano in an adjoining hall. He started with Mozart and Hayden and finished with a rousing rendition of the Beatles, "Come Together."

I won't say that the celebration provided "closure." I won't even insist that Rifka was there in spirit, even if in my son's plainspoken ability to touch people with his heart, she surely was. I will say that watching my son enveloped by tefillin for the first time, my younger son praying with devotion, my daughter chatting with a new friend (the daughter of the woman who introduced me to Rifka), listening to my American cantor cousin conducting services while my Tel Aviv cousins tried to follow along, and reuniting with friends from the accelerating decades of my life, I felt, for the first time in a long time, blessed.

A Matter of Time

Barry Lichtenberg

September 2005

In years past, once a month on Saturday night, Rifka would barricade herself in the study to write her "Home Front" column for the "Back of the Book." After a few hours, she would emerge and with a flourish hand me the draft to read. I would make some suggestions, a few of which she might incorporate into the final version, mostly, I suspect, to assuage my ego.

Rifka's columns, which spanned seven years and chronicled her life as a wife, mother, and eventually, her battle against cancer, retain their passion and immediacy. I continue to see them taped to kitchen walls and stuffed into shul tallit (prayer shawl) bags.

Now it is my turn. Once a year, the editor asks me to submit a column, if only to update Rifka's devoted fans who regularly ask after my family. It is now Saturday night and I am seated in the study writing this column against deadline, much the way Rifka did. I should be so lucky with the final product.

Rifka's first column that disclosed her illness, titled "It Takes a Village," described the myriad of ways in which our community lent a hand. The village continues to do so, with acts of kindness large and small, from shopping for my children's school clothes to high school students helping with homework to e-mails from Israel checking in.

Near the end, Rifka would tell me that my life had "chapters yet unwritten." But new chapters take time. I attend weddings and bar mitzvahs where guests speculate about the seating arrangements, and I think only of the seat that will be forever empty. Sometimes, as I drive home across the George Washington Bridge, the orange sun setting against the Palisades, the CD playing one of Rifka's favorites, Louis Armstrong's "What a Wonderful World," Rifka's absence will seem inexplicable, a cruel quirk of nature. At those moments, I struggle to grasp how the world goes on without her in it.

But our children anchor me. Our eldest celebrated his bar mitzvah two summers ago. Last summer, he attended an Israeli camp in Kfar Etzion under the auspices of the OU and returned home with the "best camper" award. We have recently celebrated the bar mitzvah of our middle son. Our youngest just turned 10 and last summer I sent her to sleep-away camp for the first time. She sent me a letter: "I am only here for two days and am already having the time of my life." The children are flourishing on the foundation that Rifka laid for them.

And I have met someone, a woman to be exact, who is helping to write the next chapter of my life.

Three years have passed. The intervening holidays for us have become a time machine that enable us not merely to recall a historical or personal event, but to relive it. Technology too has enabled us to connect with our past as never before. My children can play old videos of Rifka playing with them and hear her call their names. Sometimes, they demand to sit and watch, sometimes they cannot bear to look.

A few months ago, the Science Times had a long and dense article about the mystery of time. One physicist compared time to a loaf of bread, with each slice corresponding to a moment in time. All time, that is, all parts of the loaf (even the already consumed ones), co-exist equally and are illuminated each in their turn by the "light" of consciousness. Heavy going, I know, but I find it somehow comforting. Now I'm no physicist, but I prefer the analogy of a braided challah, a tapestry of time, with strands seeming to disappear, only to reappear in another guise, in another time.

So somewhere, Maimonides is drafting his Codex to Jewish Law. Somewhere, my grandparents have just returned from hearing Vladimir Jabotinsky on Bielanska Street in Warsaw, where he has just made his call for the "evacuation" of one million Polish Jews to Palestine. They are skeptical, but their teenage son decides that if the Germans invade, he will flee. And somewhere, Rifka sits in this study, writing her column on deadline, for all readers and for all time.

Index

Albright, Madeline, 88
Aliyah (immigration to Israel), 52, 67, 112, 150, 187-189
American Jewry, 4, 31, 55, 107, 151
Arafat, Yasser, change of attitude toward, 169, 184-5
Auschwitz, 175, 178
Bar mitzvah, 39, 196, 198
Bat mitzvah, 39, 171
Beatles, 72-73, 196
Bergen-Belsen, 118
Big Mac, Israeli kosher, ambivalent reaction to, 158
Brit Milah, 9
Burger King, 158, 160
Bush, President George W., 139, 161, 184-6
Cancer, 69, 73, 88, 116, 127, 132-134, 137, 140, 145, 161, 194, 197
Cancer time, 127
Cape Canaveral, 190-2
Chanukah, 4, 33, 79-81, 101-2, 117, 162-3, 183
Chavrusa (learning partner), 97-9
Children, 3-7, 13-5, 17-8, 20, 32-3, 39, 46-7, 49-51, 56-7, 59, 64, 67-8, 72, 76-7, 79-82, 87-92, 95-7, 99, 104-5, 108-9, 111-4, 116, 118-20, 124, 126, 128-30, 137-8, 143-5, 150-1, 155-8, 161, 163-5, 170-2, 175, 177, 179-82, 185-8, 192, 194-5, 197-8
Children, quantity of, 5-7
Christian coalition, 185
Christmas, 4, 79-81, 101-2, 162, 190
Clinton, Hillary, vindicated by Teaneck, 69
Dallas, 100-2
Daughter, birth of, 8-10
December Dilemma, 79-81
DP (displaced persons) camp, 118-20, 142
Dreams, 28, 51-2, 56, 66-7, 84, 114, 126, 150-1, 164, 178, 182, 187, 189, 191-2
Duker, Sara, 88
Egypt, seeing onself as personally redeemed from, 86-7, 105, 144, 171
Elijah, cup of, homemade, 103-4
Epstein, Helen, 19
Europe, 6-7, 18, 20, 99, 118, 155, 184-5
European Jewry, 154, 178
Faith, 75, 77, 108, 116, 129, 133-5, 137-8, 160, 170, 178
Family, 2-3, 6-8, 14-5, 18, 20-1, 28, 32-4, 50, 55-8, 62, 67, 70-1, 73, 80-2, 85-6, 89, 93-5, 100, 104, 106-7, 113-4, 116-7, 123, 127, 129-32, 134-5, 141, 145-6, 149-51, 153, 157-9, 162-3, 170-1, 173-4, 178-9, 182-3, 187, 190, 194-5, 197
"Family Newspaper", 56
Father, becoming like him politically, 184-6
Feminism, 35, 82-3, 110, 136-8
Feminism, as maternal love, 136-8
Friday, 39, 41-4, 55, 60, 70, 92-3, 124, 147, 162-3, 166, 183, 195
Friendship, 9-10, 21, 23-4, 26-9, 43, 45, 51-3, 58, 61-3, 67, 70-1, 73-4, 76, 86, 88, 93, 109, 116, 121, 123, 130-2, 134-5, 141, 146, 150, 159, 162, 178-9, 186-8, 191, 194, 196
Gender Thing, 38-40

Generations, 8, 47, 55, 84, 108, 114, 129, 140-1, 156, 171-2, 179
Germans and Germany, 87, 120, 139, 152-3, 173, 175, 184-5, 199
God, questions about, 76-8
Goetz, Mr., childhood math teacher, 11-3
Greenberg, Blu, 137
Greenberg, J.J., 137
Guilt, 58, 68, 188
Haggadah, 86-7, 103-5
Hatikvah, 47
Hebrew, 24, 55, 147, 160
High Holy Days, 112, 125, 135, 141, 147
Hitler, Adolph, 171, 177
Holidays, 33, 50-1, 75, 79-80, 83, 85-6, 101, 103-4, 114-7, 121-3, 127, 129, 139, 141, 160, 162, 171-2, 175, 198
Holocaust, 7, 18, 33, 86, 88-9, 108, 111-2, 118-9, 133-4, 140, 143, 154-6, 163, 165, 172, 178-9, 184-5, 195
Holocaust, as inheritance, 155-7
Holocaust, replenishing numbers from, 5-7
Holy Land, 158-9
Hussein, Saddam, 139-1
Ilan Ramon, 192
Inheritance (*yerusha*), 33, 144, 156
Intermarriage, 2-4, 79
International Network of Children of Jewish Holocaust Survivors, 119
Intifada, 133, 147, 188
Iraq, 139, 141, 143
Isaac (Biblical character), binding of, through a mother's eyes, 136
Israel Defense Forces, 168
Israel Emergency Solidarity Fund, 132
Israel Independence Day, 132
Israel, 50th birthday of, 106-8

Jerusalem, 82, 88, 106-7, 112, 128, 130-1, 154, 159-60, 167, 169, 179, 183, 194-5
Jessica, 2-4
Jewish education, tension between isolation and assimilation, 5-7
Jewish family, 8, 33, 93
Jewish girl, birth of, 8-10
Jewish Law, 10, 97, 199
Jewish Orthodox Feminist Alliance (JOFA), 137-8
Jewish population, small size of, 5-7
Jewish women, 8-9, 16, 29, 35, 83-4
Jewishness, 4, 100-1
Jewry, 31, 111, 154
Judaism, 3-4, 9-10, 13, 79, 106-7, 110-1, 115, 150, 166
Judenrein, 177
Kabbalah Centre, advertising strategies of, 30
Katz, Maidi, 88
Kennedy Space Center, 191
Kentucky Fried Chicken, 158
Kiddush, 39, 55, 93, 166
Kids, 3-4, 6, 11, 14-7, 20-1, 36, 39, 43, 46, 54-6, 58, 63-4, 68, 70-4, 80-1, 84, 91-2, 97, 100, 102-4, 107, 115-6, 122-5, 128, 130, 141, 145, 151, 155, 158, 160, 166-7, 170, 175-6, 179-83, 188, 190-1, 194
Land of Macs, 158-0
Levi, Coby, 88
Lichtenberg, Barry (author's husband), 3, 6, 9-10, 15-6, 20-3, 27-8, 30-1, 33, 35-7, 39, 49-50, 52, 54-5, 60-1, 65, 67-8, 71, 73, 80-2, 84, 86, 109-10, 113-4, 134, 136, 149-50, 153, 155-6, 158, 163, 167, 188-90, 194, 197
Lieberman, Joe, 164-6, 184
Little League, 125, 155
Mama, 48, 54, 72, 78, 105
Manhattan, 35, 69, 82, 181

Mark McGuire, 48
Marriage, proposed by four-year-old, 2, 4
Math, 11-3
Men, 8, 29, 31, 38-9, 52, 83-4, 99, 101, 103, 112, 137, 145, 165, 168, 191
Middle East, 7, 139, 167, 185
Mitzvah, 39, 147, 171, 196, 198
Modern Orthodox Judaism, 3, 6, 39, 51, 109, 145, 155, 187
Mom, 27-8, 42, 57-60, 81, 124
Mommy-track, 51
Motherhood, in the story of Isaac, 136-8
Mothers, 57, 59, 88-9, 136-8, 167-9
Nazis, 175, 186
New Jersey, 35, 69, 97
New Year, 94-6, 114, 124-6, 147, 162-3
New York, 5, 21, 26, 30, 42, 56, 69-70, 88, 100, 107, 110, 142, 153, 167, 180, 186
Orthodox Judaism, 3, 6, 39, 51, 82-8, 109-0, 136-7, 145, 155, 187
Palestinians, 119, 139, 167-9, 199
Parallel lives of parents and children, 49
Parents, 3-4, 6-7, 9, 17-8, 30, 32-4, 46, 49-51, 58, 63-4, 72-3, 76-7, 79-80, 88, 91, 112-5, 118-9, 123, 141, 144, 150-1, 155-7, 165, 170-1, 179, 188, 192
Passover, 4, 33, 50, 85-7, 89, 103-6, 121-3, 127, 129, 139-41, 144, 171-2, 184
Peace, 33, 52, 96, 110, 126, 135, 139, 159, 167-9, 179, 184-6
Pesach (see Passover)
Pesach Zone, the, in local supermarket, 85
Poconos, 121
Poland, 56, 68, 120, 134, 142, 173-8
pregnancy, 5

preschool, 3, 62, 124
Psalms, 10, 70, 146, 154, 173, 195
Purim, 48, 122, 127, 139
Quality time, 59, 91, 93
Rabin, Yitzhak, 110, 168, 195
Ramon, Ilan, 192
Reading room, for women's Torah study, 83-4
Reform Judaism, 109-10
Relationships, 49, 135
Remembering, 17, 23-4, 45, 47, 74, 86, 96, 102, 106, 117, 122, 131, 143, 160, 162, 164
Rice, Condoleeza, as Queen Esther, 139
Ritual, Jewish, 3, 9-10, 23, 35, 48-50, 86-7, 106, 115, 143, 153, 170
Rosensaft, Menachem, 119
Rosh HaShanah, 34, 96, 98, 112, 4-115, 125, 133
Sabbath (see *Shabbat*)
Sabbath-observant Jews, 41
Saturday, 14-5, 130, 191, 197
School, 2-4, 11-3, 15, 20-1, 23-4, 26, 41-3, 45-8, 50-1, 56-9, 61, 63, 67, 72-3, 76, 89, 91, 97, 102, 105, 110, 115, 125, 128, 130, 146, 149, 151, 159, 161, 164, 169-70, 180, 183, 187, 190, 194, 197
Seder ornaments, 103
September 11 (9/11/2001), 131, 133, 140, 147, 178, 181-3, 186
Shabbat (the Sabbath), 15, 26, 28, 41-3, 47, 49, 62, 77-8, 92-3, 95-6, 98, 106, 116-7, 127, 150, 163, 166, 175-6, 188, 195
Shanah Tova Tikatayvu, 34, 114, 126, 135, 147
Shema, 46, 179
Shiva, mourning ritual of, 10
Shoah (see Holocaust)
Shuls, 176-177
Simchat Bat, 10
Simchat Torah, 115, 160
Sleepaway Camp, 63-5
Soccer mom, 124

Sons, 2-5, 7-9, 23-4, 39-40, 45, 47-49, 54-7, 60-1, 64-5, 72, 76-8, 94-6, 98, 105, 108, 114, 121, 124-5, 136-8, 149, 155, 160, 164-7, 167-9, 172-3, 179, 191-2, 195-6, 198-9
State of Israel, 7, 90, 132, 159, 184
Stuff, 20-2, 36, 126, 162
Styles, 29-31, 182
Sukkot, 80, 112, 115, 180
Summertime, 91-3
Sundays, 29, 42-3, 51, 62, 92, 97, 110, 115, 124, 147, 155, 160, 181
Survivors, of Holocaust, in Displaced Persons camps, 19, 86, 89, 118-20, 142, 144, 154, 172
Talmud, 55, 97-8
Teaneck,N.J., 69, 88
TeaneckShuls email list, 145, 147
Terezinstadt, 192
Thanksgiving, 30, 33, 101, 115, 181
The New York Times, 30, 56, 107, 153, 167
The Wall Street Journal, 152
Time, 4, 7, 9-10, 12, 14, 16, 20-1, 25-8, 30-1, 33-7, 39, 41-2, 45-46, 51, 53-4, 56-9, 61-5, 68, 72-4, 77, 79-81, 83, 86, 91-3, 95, 97-8, 100-3, 107, 112-7, 121-3, 125-30, 133, 135, 140-2, 145, 147, 149, 151, 160-1, 163-4, 166, 170, 176, 179-86, 188-90, 192, 194-9
Tisha B'Av, 4
Torah, 39, 46, 55, 83-4, 93, 98, 115, 125, 136, 159-60, 168, 188, 192
Tower of Babel, 192
Traditions, 3, 85-6, 114, 123, 129, 170-1
Tragedy, 89, 134, 156, 161-3, 179, 183, 192
Treblinka, 120, 173-4, 177
Tu B'Shevat, 104
TV, 43, 55, 151, 164
U. S. Holocaust Memorial Museum, 118, 172

Umshlagplatz, 174
United States, 7, 135, 140, 142, 158, 164, 166, 187-8
VCR, 15, 159
Vromen, Galina, 136
War of Independence, 167
Warsaw, 89, 172-4, 177, 199
Warsaw Ghetto Uprising, 89, 172, 174
Washington, 70-1, 118, 165, 181, 198
Wedding Pages, 29-31
Weil, Simone, 19
West Bank, 184
West Side, 26
Western Wall, 159-60, 196
Wiesel, Elie, 120
Wieseltier, Leon, 55
Wild West, 101
witness, 46, 142, 144
Women, 8-9, 14-6, 29-31, 35, 38-40, 58-9, 66, 82-4, 98, 101, 112, 114-5, 136-8, 145-6, 167-9, 191
Women and Torah study, 97-9
World Trade Center, 179
World War II, 140
Writing, 50, 56, 67, 69, 142, 144, 197, 199
Writing, as bearing witness, 142-144
Writing, as father's heritage, 142-144
X-ray, 70
Y2K, 161-3
Yankees, The New York, 24, 64, 145
Yearning, 17-9, 168
Yiddish, 56, 142, 177-8
Yom Hashoah, 88, 90, 132, 143
Yom Kippur, 112, 115, 125, 160
Zionism, 106-7, 149, 151, 158, 187-8
Zornberg, Dr. Avivah, 82-83

Ben Yehuda Press presents
Jewish Women of the 20th Century

BESSIE SAINER. Bessie's "career" is full of hazards. At the age of twelve, she is exiled to Siberia because of her brothers' anti-czarist activities. At twenty-five, she loses her husband and baby girl to the ravages of civil war in revolutionary Russia.

At forty, she faces down Nazi hoodlums as she tries to disrupt a pro-Hitler rally in Madison Square Garden. At fifty-five, she is driven underground by McCarthyite persecution. At sixty-two, she squares off against racists in the South—and nearly loses the loyalty of her beloved daughter.

At eighty-eight, she is still making trouble and still making jokes.

A profoundly optimistic novel about a remarkable heroine—a rebel, a lover, a mother, a grandmother, a Jew, and an extraordinary human being.

Bessie: A Novel of Love and Revolution by **Lawrence Bush.**
ISBN# 0-9789980-3-0

HANNE GOLDSCHMIDT. Nicolette Maleckar draws upon her experiences in post-war Berlin in telling the story of Hanne, a brave-hearted waif who must find a way to begin her life in the rubble of a shattered world.

Hanne's story is a delightful rendering of the first blush of love in an impossible time. Her tale has been praised by West Virgina Public Radio for the "fairy-tale quality of the characters."

The Lilac Tree: An Enchanting Novel of Love in the Ruins of Berlin, 1945 by **Nicolette Maleckar.**
ISBN# 0-9769862-2-1

For more information, or to purchase these and other titles, visit your favorite bookstore or http://www.BenYehudaPress.com
email orders@BenYehudaPress.com

Ben Yehuda Press presents
Jewish Women of the 20th Century

DOROTHY EPSTEIN. Growing up in the immigrant communities of New York, Dorothy Epstein entered the workforce during the worst part of the Depression. The child of activists herself, Dorothy had been loathe to follow in their overburdened, impoverished footsteps.

However, fate intervened, and Dorothy soon became radicalized and spent most of her life working for the advancement of labor unions and human rights. She died in 2006 at the age of 92.
A Song of Social Significance: Memoirs of an Activist by **Dorothy Epstein.**
ISBN# 0-9769862-7-2

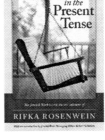

RIFKA ROSENWEIN. The daughter of Holocaust survivors, journalist Rifka Rosenwein chronicled her suburban, soccer-mom life in the back of *The Jewish Week* for seven years.

In 2001, Rifka's world was changed forever: first, like the rest of us, by the events of September 11th; and then, in a more personal blow, by a diagnosis of cancer. She died in 2003 at the age of 42.

Even when she discusses her life as being lived on "cancer time," her columns are a death-defying celebration of life. Reading her work, you can see your own friends, your parents, your children, your co-workers, your spouse... and yourself.

Life in the Present Tense: Reflections on Faith and Family by **Rifka Rosenwein.** ISBN# 0-9789980-4-9

For more information, or to purchase these and other titles, visit your favorite bookstore or http://www.BenYehudaPress.com
email orders@BenYehudaPress.com

Printed in the United Kingdom
by Lightning Source UK Ltd.
131376UK00002B/204/A